THE CHRISTIAN EXPERIENCE SERIES is for people who are interested in knowing more about their religion, and for those who have not as yet seen any reason to be interested.

Each book in the series provides material for personal thought about, and group discussion of, some basic question which concerns everyone, but is seldom discussed.

Christians are supposed to have the answers to such questions. But the answers they learned in childhood are perhaps no longer satisfactory to them or meaningful to their non-Christian neighbors.

The renewal in the Church, and the progress in modern behavioral sciences and modern philosophy, both shed new light on these basic questions:

Are suffering and death necessary as part of human life?

What is love, anyway, and how is it to be expressed?

Is God vanishing from our secular world?

How do we know that what we are doing is right?

The purpose of the series is not to offer a complete treatment of each question, or any ready answer. The purpose is, rather, to suggest lines of thought and, perhaps, action that may help the reader bring religion and life together.

The books in the Christian Experience Series are designed for use in CCD and other discussion-action groups. Each book contains eight chapters with discussion questions. Each chapter can serve as material for one meeting or two, so that the entire book may be used for an eight-week or a sixteen-week season.

General Editor, Mary Perkins Ryan

Advisory Committee, Rev. Carroll Stuhlmueller, C.P., Rev. Shawn Sheehan, Thomas E. Caulfield, M.D.

Sponsored by the National Center of the Confraternity of Christian Doctrine, 1312 Massachusetts Ave., N.W., Washington, D.C.

about loving

CHRISTIAN EXPERIENCE SERIES NO. 2

about loving

Rev. David P. O'Neill

WITNESS BOOKS

GEO. A. PFLAUM, PUBLISHER, INC.
38 WEST FIFTH STREET • DAYTON, OHIO 45402

ACKNOWLEDGEMENT

The Bible quotations in this book are from the Confraternity of Christian Doctrine translation.

PHOTO CREDITS

Cover: Fred Plaut. Page 16: John Wright. Pages 21, 28, 31, 72: Paul Tucker. Pages 35, 45, 61: UPI. Page 42: Barbara Morgan. Page 54: Ralph Looney. Page 68: John Loengard/LIFE © 1965 Time Inc. All Rights Reserved. Page 75: Ralph Crane, Black Star. Page 82: Alan Oddie. Page 89: Robert S. Halvey. Page 94: NASA, Kenneth S. Brown, Paul Tucker, RNS. Page 98: Dayton University. Page 106: Mike Willett. Page 111: INS.

NIHIL OBSTAT

Eduardus A. Connaughton
Censor Deputatus

IMPRIMATUR

†Carolus J. Alter

Archiepiscopus Cincinnatensis

Library of Congress Catalog Card Number: 66—18515

Second Printing: February 1967

Third Printing: October 1967

CONTENTS

FOREWORD

The purpose of this booklet is to help those who use it to work out, through personal thought and group discussion, their own answers to the questions: What does it mean to love? How can I love more completely and maturely?

What do we really know about how to love? Most of us are certain, perhaps, that we can recognize real love when we give it or receive it, although we could not make up a completely satisfying definition of love or loving. Yet most of us also are more or less acutely conscious of our deficiencies in loving and of not as yet having found a fully satisfying and personal answer to the meaning of love in our lives.

The causes of this state of affairs vary, of course, with each of us. But two seem to be most central and most common: first, our experience of loving may not have taught us very reliably what love is; and, second, we may never have thought of our loving as a whole, as the basic attitude of our self towards other persons, towards all reality, towards God, and so we may never have effectively tried, with God's grace, to become more loving persons.

It is easy to recognize the effects of mistaken notions of what loving means. Many mothers, for example, show what they believe to be devoted love for their children, although everyone else sees the children as being spoiled rather than loved. Many a husband gives what he thinks of as love to his wife, while she resents his apparent ignorance of the first meaning of love. Many young couples, convinced on their marriage day of their undying love for one another, find what they took to be love beginning to disappear only six months later. And many people think of themselves as loving God sincerely, while those around them find their religious devotion anxious, selfish and self-centered.

In all these cases, the failure to love can be traced, in great part at least, to previous defective experiences of love. The *Can This Marriage Be Saved* series of articles in *The Ladies' Home Journal* provides very enlightening case histories showing how people's life-experience of love deeply influences their notions of love and their power to love. This series also shows how, with wise counseling and personal effort, even people whose power to love has been seriously warped can begin to learn what loving really is and to practice it.

A part of the purpose of this booklet, then, is to examine the component elements that make up the ability to love truly and maturely. Because love has to do with the growth of personality, we shall look at the way in which human beings grow as persons, at the way in which their capacity for love expands and develops. Each chapter will sketch out the requirements of one particular period of life, in order to bring out what love should mean for us here and now, in whatever stage we have arrived. And, as we trace the development of personality and love, we shall see how love presents itself as a task, a challenge for continuing achievement throughout life, from babyhood to old age. And even beyond old age—for the Christian promise, the substance of our hope, is that our loving will go on even after we die, that death will be an entry into an intensified life of loving. When we die, we shall fall into love.

This study of the development of love should, therefore, also bring out the unity of all our loving, and help those who use this booklet to find an integrated love-meaning for their lives. We all want love and we all want to love. We may be conscious of having received true love from God and from a few human beings; we may realize that we are capable, in our better moments, of giving some love in return. But often these experiences remain separate, isolated from one another; they do not form themselves into any meaningful pattern of life. The kind of love that we receive from our parents and the kind that we give to them does not link up with our experience of falling in love. We are inclined to think of these, and the other loves that we have for brothers, sisters, and friends, as separate departments of living.

God's love for us and our love for Him can easily seem to be another department, quite separate from the natural and secular world of everyday concern. We accept His commands to love Him and our neighbor, and we put them into practice by fulfilling our "religious duties" and by trying not to hate other people. All this can seem to have little to do with our ordinary life, with its problems of "being in love," of working for a living, and of getting on well with our families and with the people down the street.

But we should experience loving, not as a series of unrelated events or relationships, but as the basic attitude of our whole self, the expression of what we are and what we are trying to become in response to love. Certainly, the affection which a girl has for her brother, for instance, seems to be a very different kind of love from the romantic love she experiences when she falls in love. But it is really the same person, the same self, who is loving in both cases. We may seem to be different with different people, but we are really the same self all the time, and our loving is not only a basic attitude of this self; in some sense it *is* this self. For love is the central value and energy of our existence.

Therefore, whether at the moment we are conscious of loving God, or our mother, or our best friend, or a difficult colleague, or a war orphan in Vietnam, our loving is still ourself. Whether it is showing itself in a prayer, a friendly smile, a warm caress, a donation, a letter of sympathy, or a lifetime of care and devotion, our loving is the same basic attitude of our being, an openness and eagerness to give and receive which must be of the essence of our real selves to be genuine. For loving is the central energy of our growth as human beings, and it is precisely at this point of central energy that God enters our lives as a living dynamism of love.

If we do not realize this most intimate connection between our loving and ourselves, and the basic unity of all our acts of loving, we cannot see clearly how to grow and mature in love. We shall not realize that, to paraphrase John Donne, every unloving act diminishes ourselves and our power to love. And neither shall we realize that making an effort to love anyone increases our total capacity to love. Many teen-agers would be surprised to learn that they could increase their capacity for adult married love by starting to love, really to love, their little brothers and sisters and by trying to be understanding and thoughtful towards their parents. Many of their elders would be equally surprised to discover that in order to love their husbands or wives or children or God more fully, they need to work at loving their in-laws and their neighbors of a different social level or racial origin. And, certainly, very few of us realize the inexhaustible riches of love for God and neighbor given us by the Holy Spirit, who pours the very love of God into our hearts.

This booklet, then, will try to help its users analyze the major elements in the growth of love in order to understand its unity, and so to discover how to grow in love and to help others do so. For this is the essence of our Christian task—to "practice the truth in love and so grow up in all things in Him who is the head, Christ" (Ephesians 4: 15).

The biblical passages at the beginning and end of each chapter are suggested as prayers to be said together before and after group discussion. The Scripture references are intended to help each reader's, and the group's, exploration of God's Word as (to quote Fr. Louis Bouyer), "the common experience of God with mankind"—an experience of love.

The questions at the end of each chapter are

meant for discussion groups, to be used in accordance with the members' common needs and common interests. But these questions are meant, too, for each reader in an individual way. They should help to make vivid, concrete and personal, thoughts which can only be outlined in a general way in a short chapter.

To most of these questions there are no clear-cut and easy answers. Many of them, again, enter areas of practical concern which are not even touched on in the text. They are meant to help each reader to think out his own answers to the meaning of love, to suggest to him the kind of questions he should be asking himself if he is to understand more deeply the meaning of his loving. Only if each reader first asks himself these questions will he be able to contribute creatively to a group discussion. Finally, of course, it is not sufficient to read about love and to talk about it; it is nothing if it is not carried into everyday living.

A bibliography is given at the end of the booklet, with some brief comments. Readers with a background of psychology may be interested in Erikson's work; they will recognize that his stages of human growth are being used as a loose framework for this booklet. Further reading may help those who use this booklet to develop, and make their own, whatever of the following ideas and themes find root in their minds. They may conclude, as I have done, that the best book about love, by far, is the Bible.

D. P. O'N.

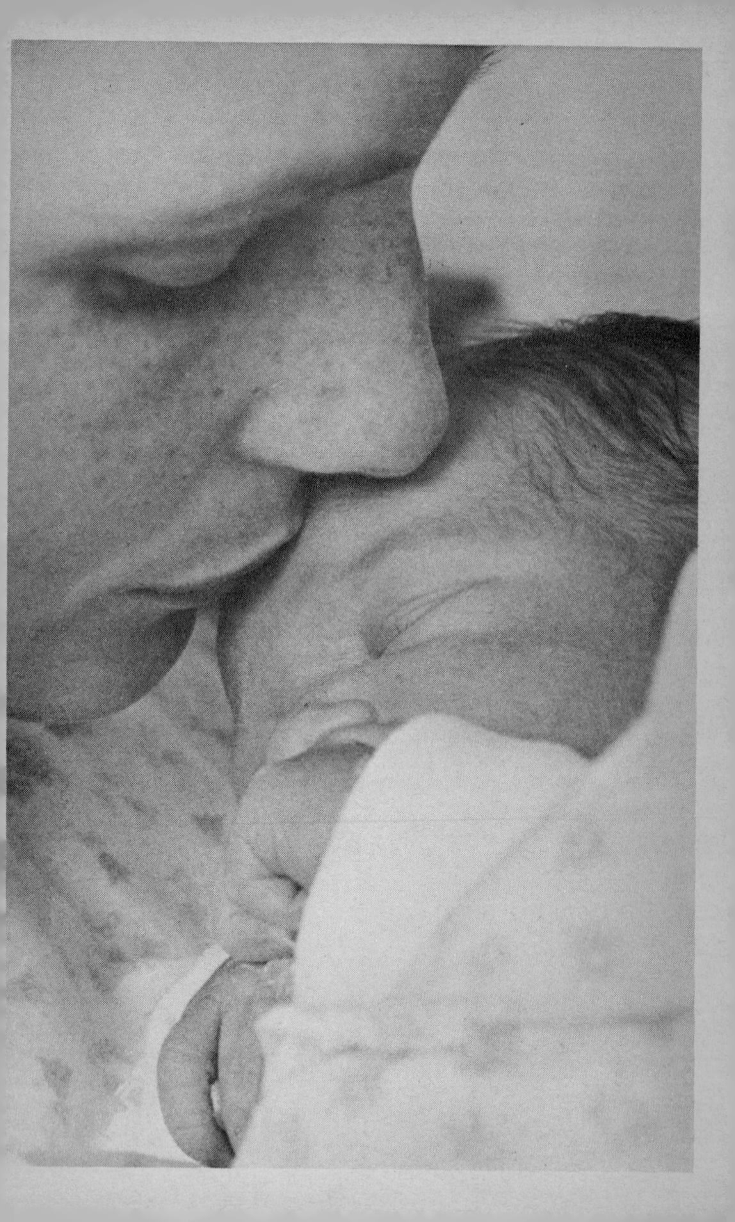

Chapter One

LOVING IS TRUSTING AND DARING

Lord, my heart is not proud,
nor are my eyes haughty;
I busy not myself with great things,
nor with things too sublime for me.
Nay rather, I have stilled and quieted
my soul like a weaned child.
Like a weaned child on its mother's lap,
so is my soul within me.
O Israel, hope in the Lord,
both now and forever.

Psalm 130

A traditional picture of love is a little baby nestling in his mother's arms; whenever we see a mother and baby, the meaning of love vividly comes home to us. The feast of Christmas, for example, makes such an immediate appeal because we sense how right it is that love should be the first human experience of the Son of Heaven come to men with His message and deeds of love.

Each person's love is meant to begin in a mother's arms. The first stirring of what will develop into love, during the first year of a baby's life, comes from his experience of being loved. He receives from his mother food and warmth, pleasure and tenderness, and a deep sense of being cared for. He learns with her a relaxed rhythm of mutual acceptance and trust, which is the basis of all human loving. When the rhythm of trust is interrupted by separating child from mother, the child very easily becomes fretful and listless; he will fail to develop physically (as well as emotionally) unless he receives ample loving attention from a substitute mother. Constant daily loving seems the only atmosphere in which a human being can really thrive.

Even in a daily atmosphere of love, however, a child cannot easily achieve this basic attitude of trust. We are all inclined, at times, to think loving is easy. Studying a baby's reactions might make us more realistic. How very frustrating his first year of life must seem to him! He becomes hungry, thirsty, cold, hot—and all he can do is cry, hoping someone will understand and help him. He is often very anxious and lonely when left on his own or with strangers, not quite sure that his mother will ever return. And so a mother who leaves a contented baby for a few days—to go to the hospital, perhaps, or a funeral—frequently returns to find her baby restless and fretful for some time.

Such experiences attack the baby's tender growth of loving trust; he very soon knows, in some dim and unformed way, the meaning of anxiety and anger, of suspicion and mistrust. Right from the beginning of human life, these two urges are at work: to love and not to love, to trust and to be suspicious, to be confident and to be anxious, to feel a sense of belonging and to feel lonely, to feel secure and to be afraid. In the face of such tensions, the baby needs the daily, almost hourly assurance of being loved, of being enfolded in the warm, sustaining arms of familiar people, where he can be certain of belonging secure. Through the love and tenderness expressed by his parents or other family members, the child will gradually achieve a strong positive balance in his feelings—he will begin to trust in love.

When he senses trustfulness in the love of those around him the little child begins to develop a sense of being trustworthy. In the growth of love we constantly find this same dialogue—trust begets trust, and love begets love. The child absorbs into himself and makes his own the love-attitudes of those around him. From the tenderness, warmth and loving confidence he senses in them, he gradually learns his first lesson of loving. He begins to reach out beyond himself with a trustful confidence secure enough to overcome his anxieties, his frustrations, his suspicions.

These negative feelings may, indeed, become dominant from time to time during the child's first years. When a strange relative swoops down upon him, for example, or an over-friendly dog knocks him over, the child quickly retreats to his father and mother. But if his parents have loved him enough, his basic confidence in himself, in people, and in things will not be overpowered by negative experiences. He will overcome them and continue to develop a firm attitude of loving trust. Helping him to gain such an attitude should be the primary concern of parents during his babyhood days and thereafter, because during these years the foundations are laid for his further growth in love. When, in adolescence, he begins to take over the responsibility for his own growth in love, this development must always include growth in the primary aspect of trust, and continue all through life. For each stage of life brings a new demand for a trustful, daring, reaching out into love.

Most of us can recognize in our adult selves the same positive and negative tendencies that we see in babies. We do want to love and be loved; yet even with those people whom we dearly want to love, we find ourselves sometimes doubtful and hesitant. We wonder whether they really appreciate us, really care for us. We are hurt at their lack of consideration; we may sometimes be conscious of an unreasonable desire to hurt them in return. Even

when they are showing us affection, we suspect their real motives, or are nagged by anxiety that this situation is too good to last.

To love another is to leap over these negative feelings; it is always in some sense truly a leap in the dark. We must let ourselves go with trusting confidence into the unknown reality of the other person, with faith in him, in his essential goodness. We must dare to believe in the reality of the love, the warmth of heart, that he offers us. We must dare to be dependent on the love of another, to admit that we are not sufficient for ourselves.

This deep level of faith in others—this being prepared to let ourselves go out in trusting, confident love—is a continuing challenge through life, and more of a challenge to some than to others. As the baby learns to walk around and meet new persons, he has to build on the faith he has in his parents and so learn to trust new friends. The same thing is true of the child when he enters adolescence, and of the adolescent as he becomes a man. At each stage, we have to attain a deeper level of trust if we are to grow in love.

Of course, all of us find—sooner or later and more or less frequently—that our trust in some other person seems to have been misplaced or even betrayed. If we are firmly grounded in a basic attitude of trust in people, we dare to go on and love again. We gain prudence in the way we offer love and open ourselves to love without shutting ourselves up in cautious fear. Still more, as we mature in love, we come to realize that faith in another person must, ultimately, be based on faith in God's love for him and in his potentialities to become the person God intends him to be. When we reach this level of faith in others, our trust can never really be betrayed.

The tension of faith and suspicion, of trust and mistrust, reaches a peak and takes on the quality of great achievement or high tragedy in the closest of human relationships—marriage. The daily friction of life together, with its opportunities for mutual suspicion, anxiety and rivalry, needs to be caught up into, and enriched by, deep, trusting faith in one another if married life is to be worth living. A readiness to be daring and to love wholeheartedly is needed to give meaning and purpose to the daily reality of common life and to the daily tenderness of married love. Above all, this attitude of loving faith and mutual trust is the essential foundation for the joyful, uninhibited self-giving which can make sexual intercourse so fruitful in the growth of personality, so enriching as a dedication of married love.

This kind of deep faith in another person, this attitude of complete trusting love, is what the Bible means by faith in God. (The dictionary itself gives "to trust, confide in" as the meaning of the Latin word *fidere* from which our word *faith* is derived.) Too often we think of our faith in God as a matter of intellect only—we believe that God exists, we believe in the statements of the Apostles' Creed. But Christian faith means rather that we believe *in* God, the Father, the Son and the Spirit, as persons, and this is the basis on which we believe *what* God has revealed. A purely intellectual faith would be no different from our belief in what mathematicians or biologists tell us. Christian faith is something more.

St. Paul tells us that we believe with our hearts; he tells us that the message of holiness "is near thee, in thy mouth and in thy heart (that is, the word of faith which we preach). For if thou confess with thy mouth that Jesus is the Lord, and believe in thy heart that God has raised him from the dead, thou shalt be saved. For with the heart a man believes unto justice" (Romans 10: 8-11).

Consider the loving faith and trusting heart of Abraham, the father of the people of God. Reading the colorful account of his life (Genesis 12-25), we see, again and again, his attitude of confidence in God's love, in God's promise that Abraham would be the father of God's own people. He was a wandering nomad most of his life, the husband of a childless marriage, a man without a country. Yet he had a deep sense of belonging to God, of being the message-bearer of a covenant of love and trust between God and the people who would grow from his Son.

God continually asked His people to trust in His covenant of love. Often they failed Him. The trust God sought and sometimes received is beautifully expressed in many of the Psalms, such as 130 (given at the beginning of this chapter), 120, and 21, the trusting prayer that Jesus prayed to His Father as He was dying on the cross. The whole life of Our Lord and, above all, His death and resurrection, give us the perfect example of total trust and confident faith in the Father.

This faith Jesus has won for us and offers us as a free gift. If we accept it with open hearts, our whole scale of values will be raised. Our prayer, for example, will become less of a frantic "Gimme!" and more of a trustful presentation of our needs to our Father. When our prayers do not seem to be heard, we shall not be disturbed but continue in our trust in Him who knows our needs better than we do. Our trustful love will help us to have faith even when doubts come into our minds about God and what we believe, when we feel suspicious of the love of others, when we seem to lose trust even in ourselves. Our faith will no longer be dependent on anything or anyone except the love of God given us in Christ.

For, as love comes to us in the beginning of life from the experience of being loved, so the power of loving God and other people will continue to grow in us if we let ourselves be open to the experience of God's love, and accept with open hearts His gift of trusting faith. As St. John tells us, "If we love one another, God abides in us, and his love is perfected in us" (1 John 4: 12).

READINGS: Psalms 21, 24, 26; Romans 4; Hebrews 11.

DISCUSSION QUESTIONS

How can people who have not gained a good sense of basic trust in childhood go about cultivating it in adolescence or adulthood?

How might children who are living under conditions that stifle the growth of this basic trust be helped to gain it? How might such adolescents and adults be helped? Do you think that society—if it is to be healthy—needs to provide such help, somehow?

Do you think that basic trustfulness has any relevance in the interracial situation of your town or city?

How might this attitude of love be applied in international situations—with other major powers? with small nations? with emerging nations? Do you think this is an impractical ideal?

Do you think it is possible to have a trusting attitude of faith in God without having basic trust in the people around us?

In the Canon of the Mass, we ask God to accept our offering as He once accepted that of our Patriarch, Abraham. What do you think this has to do with the way you take part in Sunday Mass?

I lift up my eyes toward the mountains;
whence shall help come to me?
My help is from the Lord,
who made heaven and earth.
May he not suffer your foot to slip;
may he slumber not who guards you;
Indeed he neither slumbers nor sleeps,
the guardian of Israel.
The Lord is your guardian; the Lord is your shade;
he is beside you at your right hand.
The sun shall not harm you by day,
nor the moon by night.

The Lord will guard you from all evil;
he will guard your life.
The Lord will guard your coming and your
going, both now and forever.

Psalm 120

Chapter Two

LOVING IS BECOMING A PERSON

Beloved, let us love one another, for love is from God. And everyone who loves is born of God, and knows God. He who does not love does not know God; for God is love. In this has the love of God been shown in our case, that God has sent his only-begotten Son into the world that we may live through him. In this is the love, not that we have loved God, but that he has first loved us, and sent his Son a propitiation for our sins. Beloved, if God has so loved us, we also ought to love one another.

John 4: 7-11

By the time a baby begins to walk and talk, he is beginning to be conscious of himself in a new way. The very shape of his world is different when he stands on his own feet. He is able to move around, to do things, to have things, just because he wants to. He discovers the meaning of "me" and "mine." He learns the power that his loud "No!" to a command or suggestion gives him to disturb the magic omnipotence of his parents. He is beginning to experience the meaning of being a self, a real person.

As he tries out this exciting sense of being himself, of being able to go as he pleases, to decide things, to give or to hold back, to keep or to throw away, to say "yes" or "no," he is keenly aware of his parents' attitude to this new self. For in stepping out on his own, he is leaving behind the warm, trustful security of being a lovable little baby who can do no wrong.

Every time we go forward to a new level of loving, we experience this same sense of leaving behind the old familiar security; we must let the old ways die in order that the new ones may come to life. We seem to die a little every time we grow a little. The uncertainty of any new growth in love often makes the old ways seem preferable. After a toddler is growled at because of a stormy display of independence, for instance, he will cuddle up to his mother to be her little baby again. His mother, too, after

his wanderings and tantrums, may also be longing for the quieter days of six months ago when loving him was easier.

But only if a child senses that his mother and father's love is unfailing, even in the face of his willful and naughty behavior, will he come to realize he has lost nothing by his step forward. He should find the loving trust and warm security of his babyhood still intact, but now enriched by his new independence and consciousness of himself. Such growth in love enables the child to realize, in however unformed a way, the great truth that whenever we begin to love at a higher level of growth, we are able to regain all that we feel we have left behind, and to find there new riches and satisfactions.

Whenever we are loved, we absorb the attitudes and values of those who are loving us; what we receive as a gift from them seems to come alive in us. So the child, sensing his parents' unfailing love in his selfhood, finds their love-attitudes coming alive in himself. If he were able to reason it out, he might say, "I am being loved all the time, even when I am naughty, so I must be lovable in my real self." He gathers that he is being loved for what he is, rather than for what he may be doing, saying or deciding at any moment. He begins to sense that he is worth loving, and that his gift of himself in love will be welcomed as something worthwhile. And so he comes to experience the joy of love-giving.

If his parents' love shows itself in an easy tolerance of his efforts toward independence combined with a firm control when necessary, he will also be absorbing these values into his own self-love and self-understanding. He will be gaining the beginnings of a self-attitude of balanced tolerance and control. All these childhood "attitudes" are, of course, in the budding stage; sometimes they seem so nebulous as to defy description in words. But they are vitally important to the child's development; they are the building-blocks of his self-confidence, and of his capacity to love himself and to love others.

Just as with his growth in trustfulness as a baby, the growth of this sense of becoming a real person, self-confident and lovable, is never smooth and easy. The child finds many things far beyond his strength and ability. He is often stopped, corrected, and sometimes punished; his exciting activities must frequently give way to the time schedule of meals, bed, and being washed; he discovers the aggressiveness and heartlessness of other children, especially those a little older than he. Many times he collapses in tears, or runs to his mother. Through all these experiences, he comes to know anger, jealousy, self-disgust. But perhaps the word "shame" best sums up the negative tendency of this stage in growth.

Shame is a feeling of our own worthlessness, a desire to hide ourselves from the view of others, even from our own view; we feel the urge to sink into the ground out of sight. A person who is deeply and habitually ashamed of himself often will form a false self. He will wear a mask which serves, as long as he lives at a shallow level, to hide what he considers his worthless real self.

This kind of basic shame makes loving almost impossible. When someone cannot believe in his own lovableness, he cannot see how another could sincerely love him just for himself. He cannot accept love, and feels unworthy to give in love. This is why every little child needs to feel the constant certainty of being loved, of receiving for his very own self a warm affection that is reliable and unchangeable. Otherwise, this basic shame may damage his possibilities of growth in love.

All of us, at times, feel this tension between self-confidence and shame, for it continues to a greater or lesser extent throughout our lives. We may have such moody thoughts as "no one would like me if they knew what I was really like inside." Sometimes, when large or even small things go wrong with us, we experience a deep attack on our self-confidence, causing us to close ourselves off from others and hug our shame to ourselves.

Our only way back to love is through our own acceptance of our true selves, and through recognizing that others do love us for what we really are. For only by being open to the experience of love can we come to appreciate our own essential dignity and lovableness as persons.

The need of the child for unfailing love shows us why the message of God's unfailing love for us is such a wonderful gift—a gift that can overcome our shame and open us up to love. God knows us for what we really are, yet He loves us. He answers, too, our instinctive need for total love. However good our parents, however kind our friends, however loving our husband or wife, they are never

perfect; often they are far from perfect. They can never fill our deep need for love. As St. Augustine said, God has made us for Himself, and our hearts cannot rest until they rest in Him.

The whole Bible gives us the message of God's realistic love for us. He chose, among rebellious men, the descendants of Abraham to be His own people, bound to Him by a love-covenant. Not only did He care for them during the waiting time with a never-failing love but, through Moses and the prophets, He put before them constantly the meaning of their failure to be faithful in love. They were constantly confronted with God's demand for total love. Moses summed it up for the people in terms later re-emphasized by Jesus: "Hear, O Israel! The Lord is our God, the Lord alone. Therefore, you shall love the Lord, your God, with all your heart, and with all your soul, and with all your strength" (Deuteronomy 6: 4-5).

If the demand of total loving seemed difficult to the Israelites (as, indeed, it still does to us when we really think of it), the answer came in the promised Messiah. The Son of God came to live a human life to the full capacity of love, to give us the love-sign of His death and new life after death. Christ's total gift of Himself in love heals all of us, who are open to receive Him, of our love-failure and shame, and His love shows us the way to a new life in the Spirit, to a new level of loving.

For the message of divine love is not only addressed to all men, but to each of us personally. The Bible makes this wonderful truth clear in all God's dealings with individual men and women. Our Lord accepted each person as he was at the moment (e.g., the episode of the Samaritan woman, John 4). And so He does with each of us, challenging us to grow in love, to cooperate with Him in becoming the full person God wants each of us to be. He enables us to set aside our mask and pretense in a full acceptance of truth, to break out of our self-centeredness into a total commitment to love.

We need to realize, more clearly than many of us do, that Christ's gift of love, which makes possible a new life, is not given us because of any good that we have done, or because we pray to God or show love to Him. Christ loves us simply because we are ourselves.

St. John insists, in his first Epistle, that it is God who has first loved us. God knows us personally, and has shown His love for us in the gift of His Son. Through the Son, we are able to know God, to enter into a personal relationship of love with Him, and to achieve in this relation ship our full growth as persons. St. John goes on to show us how we can make a great leap forward in our understanding of this personal relationship between God and ourselves when he tells us simply: "God is love, and he who abides in love, abides in God, and God in him . . . . There is no fear in love; but perfect love casts out fear" (1 John 4: 16-18).

We must try to accept the message of divine love with full trust and confidence, making our own the conviction that God's unchanging love is offered, not only to God's people as a whole, but to each of us personally. Each time we go to Mass, we hear some aspect of this message as Christ speaks to us through the inspired words of the Epistle and Gospel. Again, we may hear it whenever we prayerfully read the Bible. By opening ourselves to the message of God's unfailing love and standing invitation to know and love Him, we can begin to gain a real understanding of our own personal value, our dignity, our essential lovableness. And, just as little children absorb the values and attitudes of those who love them, we can be absorbing and making our own the divine ideals and fully mature human love we see in Christ.

The more we allow this greatest of all loves to be alive within us, the less will we fear being ourselves, revealing ourselves as we really are. We shall try to be our true selves with God—in prayer, for example, and in Confession, not worrying about whether we are feeling pious or not. And we shall also try to be our true selves with those whom we want to love.

So we will experience the deep self-transformation which true loving works in us, as it does in little children. We will grow in the knowledge of being a person and discover the true self-confidence and security of love. Our cooperation with this gift of divine love will lead us into the new life Jesus promises us. Through the energy of this new life of divine love, we shall return to all our human loves, cares, and concerns, and find them all enriched with a higher meaning and value.

READINGS: Psalms 135, 102; Romans 8: 31-39; 1 John 4: 7-21.

DISCUSSION QUESTIONS

Do you think it possible for parents to communicate a greater sense of personal value and dignity to their children than they have themselves?

Where and how should the process begin of helping the members of underprivileged groups to attain a sense of personal value and dignity?

How does a lack of self-value and of self-confidence affect the love-relationship of marriage?

If you were teaching religion to a group of children in a city slum or in a migrant worker camp, how would you try to convince them of God's love for them?

How should our response to God's gift of love help us to be more loving to those in our family and immediate social circle? Toward outgroups in our community?

How might our trusting acceptance of God's love for us in Christ help us toward a more realistic view of ourselves?

> *No one has ever seen God. If we love one another, God abides in us and his love is perfected in us. In this we know that we abide in him and he in us, because he has given us of his Spirit. And we have seen and do testify, that the Father has sent his Son to be Savior of the world. Whoever confesses that Jesus is the Son of God, God abides in him and he in God. And we have come to know, and have believed, the love that God has in our behalf. God is love, and he who abides in love abides in God, and*

God in him. In this is love perfected with us, that we may have confidence in the day of judgment; because as he is, even so are we also in this world. There is no fear in love; but perfect love casts out fear, because fear brings punishment. And he who fears is not perfected in love. Let us therefore love, because God first loved us.

1 John 4: 12-19

Chapter Three

LOVING IS A JOY

Sing joyfully to the Lord, all you lands;
serve the Lord with gladness;
come before him with joyful song.
Know that the Lord is God;
he made us, his we are;
his people, the flock he tends.
Enter his gates with thanksgiving,
his courts with praise;
Give thanks to him; bless his name, for he is good:
the Lord, whose kindness endures forever,
and his faithfulness, to all generations.

Psalm 99

One afternoon in New Zealand, I believe I discovered something of the joy of the Lord's creation. It was a still, sunny day after a winter storm, with a transparent clarity in the air. I took a long walk, reaching a peak some fifteen hundred feet above the seashore. There, in the calm, brilliant sunshine, I looked at the beauty God has fashioned in this island home of mine in the southern ocean. A few miles away, and far below me, beaches stretched out on either side. Fifty miles up the coast, high mountains were shining with snow from the storm. Out over the ocean a handful of little islands sparkled in the sun, and beyond a larger island with snowy peaks.

I looked for a long time, laughing for joy at such beauty and wonder. I think I understood a little of what God felt when He looked at all He had made, and saw that it was good. I was, however, still well aware that this golden ocean could be cruel, that the deep shadows through the hills were the fault lines of old earthquakes that might be reactivated at any moment, that the city far below on the bay was as full of loneliness and sin as cities usually are. But yet I felt a sense of joy, a realization that creation is a work of love.

We are often so solemn about love that we forget love is a joy, a thing to wonder at and to laugh about. I saw this joy one day recently when I took

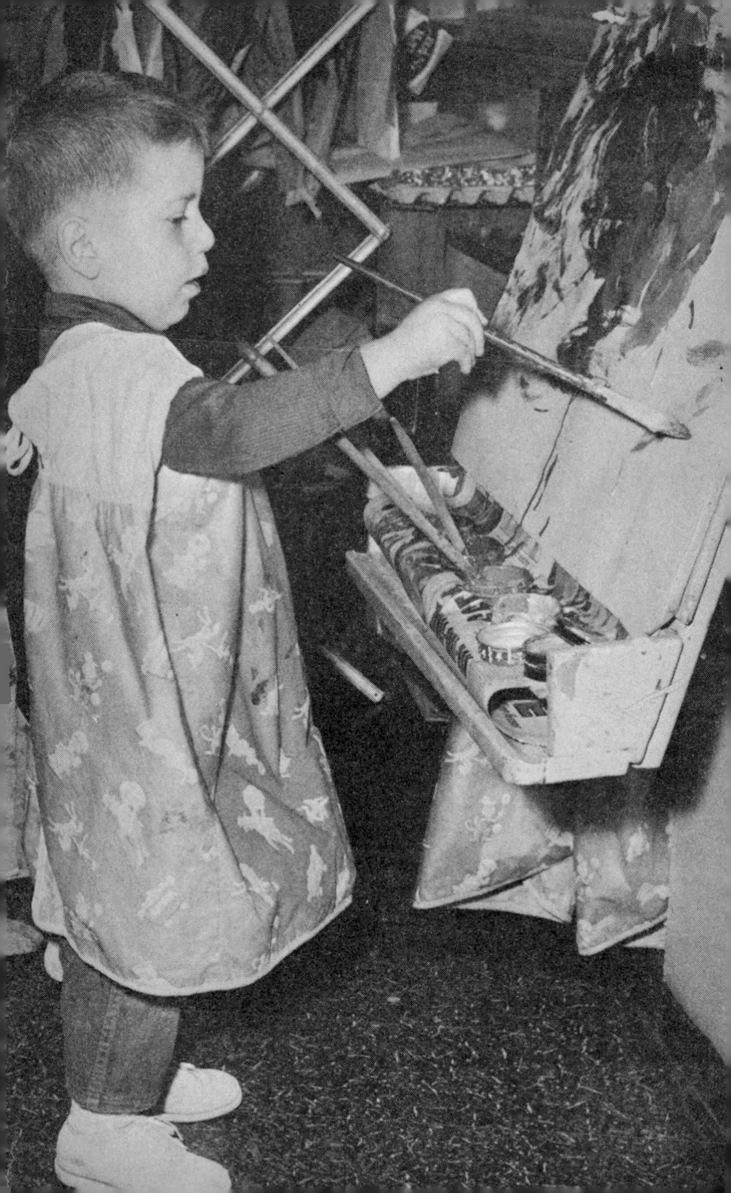

my four-year-old niece for a swim on one of our ocean beaches. She stood, holding my hand for safety, where the farthest reach of the thundering surf would just touch her feet, and she laughed aloud at the sheer joy and fun of all the noise and light and moving water. She was loving life itself, and all the new possibilities life was offering her—the joy of wading in the surf, the joy of shaping wet sand into houses and castles, the joy of discovering quaint shapes and forms in the driftwood along the tide-line.

This niece of mine is at the age when a child is reaching out into the world of reality and finding it good and joyful; this age is one of widening initiative, of discovery and enterprise. Ideally, with his sense of basic trustfulness and his sense of being himself well established, a child should at this stage go on and find that the whole of reality can be fun, that he can love all that is.

Parents should be particularly alert, then, to encourage the child of this age to use his initiative and to be joyfully creative. A child should be given wide outlets for creativity, in his contacts with nature, his handling of simple things like wood, sand, clay, and water. He should begin to learn the excitement of color, line and shape, both from his own drawing, painting and modeling, and also from adults appreciation of his creations. All these experiences, as well as those provided by different kinds of toys, by picture-books and new words, will lead him to develop an attitude of loving enjoyment of things and people.

A preschool child must also begin to recognize

that he cannot have anybody's love, even his mother's, as his exclusive possession. As his understanding of his family deepens, he finds even her love, which seemed centered on him, really shared with his father, his brothers and sisters and, perhaps, a new baby. Nor does he find himself the center of his father's love.

These experiences should, ideally, introduce him to the essential lesson that loving involves sharing and generosity. He should begin to realize, in however unformed a way, that his enjoyment of the things he holds dear, the things he makes and even the people he loves, can never be complete if he clings to them for himself only. He is facing the demand of love to share, to let go of something treasured for oneself. He should begin to respond to love's demand of joyful generosity.

But if he is to recognize this demand for what it is and to begin to respond to it, he must—as always—absorb this love-attitude mainly from his parents. He must be able to sense the generosity of their love for one another, and also of their love for him. For they too are faced with love's demand to be generous in giving up many satisfactions of their protective love for their child, in order to give him more and more room to grow. They must give up more of the satisfactions of doing things for him, so that he can grow in initiative and creative joy. They must allow him to run more freely, to reach out into a wider world. In other words, they must be truly generous if their love is not to smother and dominate the child's new growth.

Recently I visited a family I was counseling. In

the course of our conversation, the wife picked up her five-year-old boy and started cuddling him like a baby. Then she asked him, "Whose little boy are you?" Her effort to show me that the boy loved her better than his father ended in confusion when the child replied, "I'm nobody's little boy. I'm mine!" The child could only completely reject this kind of possessive love, which was using and exploiting him rather than treating him as a person.

Children very easily absorb the negative attitudes of such parents, attitudes which destroy the joy and generosity of love. Again, adults who are forgetful of the deep needs and desires of children tend to ignore them as persons—an attitude which can seem to a child to be cold, even rejecting. Being treated as a thing, rather than as a person, can deepen in the child a sense of lonely insecurity, a feeling that all is not well with his world, a basic uneasiness which comes to be focused on himself, his thoughts, feelings and actions—an uneasiness which can be the prime enemy of his capacity for joyful love.

All of us suffer to some extent from this kind of inner tension which stunts a person's growth into the full joy of loving. If we do not recognize it and try to overcome it, this basic uneasiness remains a strong negative force below our conscious level of activity, daily attacking our capacity for active loving. It can even cast a gloom over our attempts to love; we may have a vague feeling of something wrong and forbidden whenever we really begin to enjoy any relationship. We may belong to that large class of people who are not content unless they are worried about something.

Many of us, in the anxious self-importance of later years, set aside too easily the playfulness of childhood. We think of loving as a methodical and difficult task, rather than a joyful exuberance of being. Perhaps this is a little of what the Lord Jesus meant when He told us to discover the meaning of childhood again if we want to enter the kingdom of love.

Being childlike does not mean, of course, that loving should be based on a romantic, fairy-tale view of life. We should not try to exclude from our awareness the negative forces and tensions that psychologists study and try to deal with, the things that wise men of earlier times called the effects of original sin. If we are realistic with ourselves, recognizing our pettinesses and struggles as well as our ideals, we can find some antidote to our worried self-importance. We can accept love only when we can laugh at ourselves a little.

Certainly, when two human beings love one another, they should share one another's laughter and joy. Whenever we experience beauty and wonder and goodness, whether on a mountaintop, a seashore, or in another person, we should open ourselves to the joy of love—sharing a little in God's joy. Even when we are most keenly conscious of what is negative in our lives, of all our failures to love, our pain, frustration, anxiety, we can always be conscious too of the positive power of love and joy as the dominant meaning of our lives. For God has put into His whole creation the meaning of joyful love. He has renewed joyful love in human life by leading us back into love through the Redemption.

On the very night of His passion, the night of betrayal and desertion, when all the loneliness, anxiety and hatred of men were centered on Him, Jesus spoke to His followers about the full joy of loving. "As the Father has loved me," He told them, "I also have loved you. Abide in my love. If you keep my commandments you will abide in my love, as I also have kept my Father's commandments, and abide in his love. These things I have spoken to you that my joy may be in you, and that your joy may be made full" (John 15: 9-12).

On this same dark night, Jesus promised us the gift of the Spirit, to continue His work of truth and love. This Spirit, the vital energy of the Father and Son in person, is spoken of on the first page of the Bible as the creative breath of God stirring over the dark waters of an empty world. He is the truth-giving inspiration of the sages and prophets who gathered the whole Bible story together, with its theme of a love-dialogue of God with men. It is this Spirit which the Risen Christ gave to His Church community under the signs of wind and fire to remain with it forever.

The same Spirit comes as a free gift to each of us, pouring the love of God into our hearts. He dwells in the deep center of our being as a vital energy of love and joy and truth. St. Paul, describing the effects of the Spirit, the qualities of a life lived in the Spirit, begins with love and joy (Galatians 5: 22-23). We all know at least one or two people who radiate this joy (which is quite different from a forced and irritating cheerfulness) even in the most adverse and painful circumstances; we feel warmed and strengthened when we meet them. But all Christians are meant thus to witness to the gift of the Spirit, and we too can come to do so if we cooperate with His work of freeing us from our self-concern, freeing us for the joy of loving.

READINGS: Psalms 32, 62, 103; Galatians 5: 16-26; Philippians 3: 4-9.

DISCUSSION QUESTIONS

Have we a right to be joyful when so many people are lacking in the minimum conditions for human happiness? If so, why and under what conditions?

Why are "Operation Headstart" and similar programs so important in connection with the phase of development described in this chapter?

How does the habit of laughing at our own absurdity help us to love God? To love other people?

Why do we call the Holy Spirit the Spirit of love? In what way do you experience His "abiding" in your life?

How does our tendency to be basically anxious and uneasy about life hamper our efforts to love others? How does the message of our Redemption help us in dealing with this problem?

In what sense should life be fun? Should loving always be a joyful experience?

How does our own growth in personal initiative help us to respect and enjoy the differences in the personalities of others?

Having been justified therefore by faith, let us have peace with God through our Lord Jesus Christ, through whom we also have access by faith unto that grace in which we stand, and exult in the hope of the glory of the sons of God. And not only this, but we exult in tribulations also, knowing that tribulation works our endurance, and endurance tries virtue, and tried virtue hope. And hope does not disappoint, because the charity of God is poured forth in our us.

Romans 5: 1-5

Chapter Four

LOVING IS CARING

The Lord is my shepherd; I shall not want.
In verdant pastures he gives me repose;
Beside restful waters he leads me;
he refreshes my soul.

He guides me in right paths
for his name's sake.
Even though I walk in the dark valley
I fear no evil; for you are at my side
With your rod and your staff
that give me courage.

You spread the table before me
in the sight of my foes;
You anoint my head with oil;
my cup overflows.
Only goodness and kindness follow me
all the days of my life;
And I shall dwell in the house of the Lord
for years to come.

Psalm 22

The Lord as the good shepherd of His people, guiding and guarding them with loving care, is a familiar theme throughout the Bible. Jesus used it on several occasions to explain His own work here on earth; the shepherd and sheepfold image provides the context of His statement of His mission: "I came that they may have life, and have it more abundantly." It shows us very vividly something always present in love—an urge to care for those we love, to be dedicated and committed to their well-being, to work for their happiness.

Such love does not come easy. We often speak of a difficult task to which we are dedicated and which provides joyful satisfaction as "a labor of love." So when two people love one another, their mutual love must involve them in slowly and patiently building together an open realm of mutual care and joy.

An active element of loving normally should begin to be part of a child's life when he goes to school and enters the world of formal learning. His ability to labor in love should grow through his grade-school years, together with his sense of satisfaction in the task well done.

Of course, he should have been showing an appetite for work and learning before he went to school. A child of six and seven asks endless questions about the how and why and what of things and people. He wants, too, to be working; he delights to "help" his father and mother with their real tasks. He is no longer fully satisfied with the world of play, exciting as the play-world is with all its elements of fun and fantasy, of learning the shape of reality, of mastering skills and facing new problems of personal experience. He begins to want to be doing things that provide a satisfaction and service to others as well as himself. Rightly guided, he can experience a new joy in life, the joy of the task well done, of completing something of more lasting and other-related value than a house of blocks or a picture in the sand.

At this stage of development, therefore, the child should begin to learn that being related to others in love requires him to work, to learn, to care—though fully to grasp this lesson is, of course, a lifetime task. A child's interest in accomplishment is only sporadic; his personal interest is still basically centered on himself and his needs. Again, his sense of time and the future is still undeveloped; immediate needs and pleasures set up a strong demand not yet counterbalanced by a clear idea of future and more lasting satisfactions. As the child develops a longer view of time, he becomes more able to postpone or completely bypass his immediate pleasure in favor of higher values in the future for himself and for others also. This progressive understanding of time and, eventually, of what is beyond time, is one of the marks of growing maturity.

A child does not always find it easy to grapple with his tasks of learning and working, involving him as they do also in new relationships with teachers and fellow students as well as with members of his family. Very often, too, he cannot easily perceive any immediate meaning in what he is told to do. He does not see the reason to write clearly, for example, let alone to spell correctly. Much of what he is asked to do has meaning only in terms of a long view of his eventual life tasks and of his capacity for mature love and dedication later on.

A child is fortunate, then, if his parents are themselves mature enough to pass on to him some support and encouragement and, even more, a living example of the mature values of learning, working, and caring. Many adults seem to have given up the struggle to meet love's demand of dedication and care, to be carried out through work, study and personal responsibility; their lives seem to be based on the grasping of shallow, day-to-day pleasures, on securing immediate satisfactions in a way proper only to early childhood. The lives of such people reflect an apathy and listlessness towards the deeper needs both of themselves and others. They cannot make any efforts to accomplish tasks of long-term value.

The child of parents such as these will find his task harder, as will the child of parents who feel themselves failures and are determined that he is not going to repeat their failure. Such parents tend to emphasize the importance of work and learning, without giving their child anything of the love-meaning behind stern duty. A child can also be easily over-burdened by well-meaning parents with a strong religious sense, who attempt to emphasize his "religious duty" to work, study and be obedient, giving it the religious sanctions of sin, judgment, and hell.

In all such cases, a child's development becomes, instead of an exciting and challenging step forward in love, a heavy burden that often seems beyond his strength. Although the work he "must" do seems crushing and meaningless, his failure to meet its challenge may leave him with an uneasy feeling of personal failure and guilt, often reinforced by the blaming and shamming efforts of the adults around him. He may easily lapse into attitudes of listless apathy or shrewd expedience. He may say to himself, "What's the use? I don't care anyway!"

Yet late childhood—the grade school years—should be the very period when a child learns to care. Through his deepening friendships and family bonds, he should gain a real sense of the meaning and value of persons; he should slowly grow to understand that his regard for others commits him to loyalty, responsibility, care and obedience. He should begin to feel that his occasional failures to be kind, careful, respectful, generous, and forgiving, are really failures to love.

Thus recognizing the inadequacy of one's love signals the budding of a true personal conscience, having an effect quite different from the habitual sense of uneasy guilt described earlier. Because this sense of inadequacy is based on a growing sense of personal value, and on the positive, forward urging of love, it brings the light of self-meaning into the child's life, rather than anxiety and confusion. This growth of conscience, based on personal values of love, leads the child to understand that God's intimate love for him demands of him active loving and forward growth. Simultaneously, he develops a sense of sin in the Christian sense, as a refusal of love, a running away from love.

A Christian conscience, undistorted by adult efforts to awaken the sense of sin prematurely or stunted by faulty moral training at the preliminary superego stage, should be a force of peace, confidence and security, stimulating the young person to grow in responsibility, care, and self-commitment. Love and dedication now become matters of true personal decision. He better understands the love-meaning behind his daily tasks of work, learning, and personal service.

In thinking about and discussing these themes of human growth in love, most of us become conscious of our need to work on each of these aspects of loving. Even if each of them had entered into our personal development at the ideal stage in the ideal way, our growth in love would still be a never-ending task. Love is never a static achievement, but always a living energy, forward-moving. We should never feel fully satisfied, never cease to see a need for further growth, because love has no ending but goes on into infinity.

We must always seek growth in love, for God Himself is love. He comes to make His home in our hearts, calling us to a decision for a life-dedication to love. When Jesus was asked what we must do to inherit eternal life, He quoted from the Old Testament: "Thou shalt love the Lord they God with thy whole heart, and with they whole soul, and with thy whole strength, and with they whole mind; and thy neighbor as thyself" (Luke 10: 27).

Love of God and neighbor calls us to self-giving

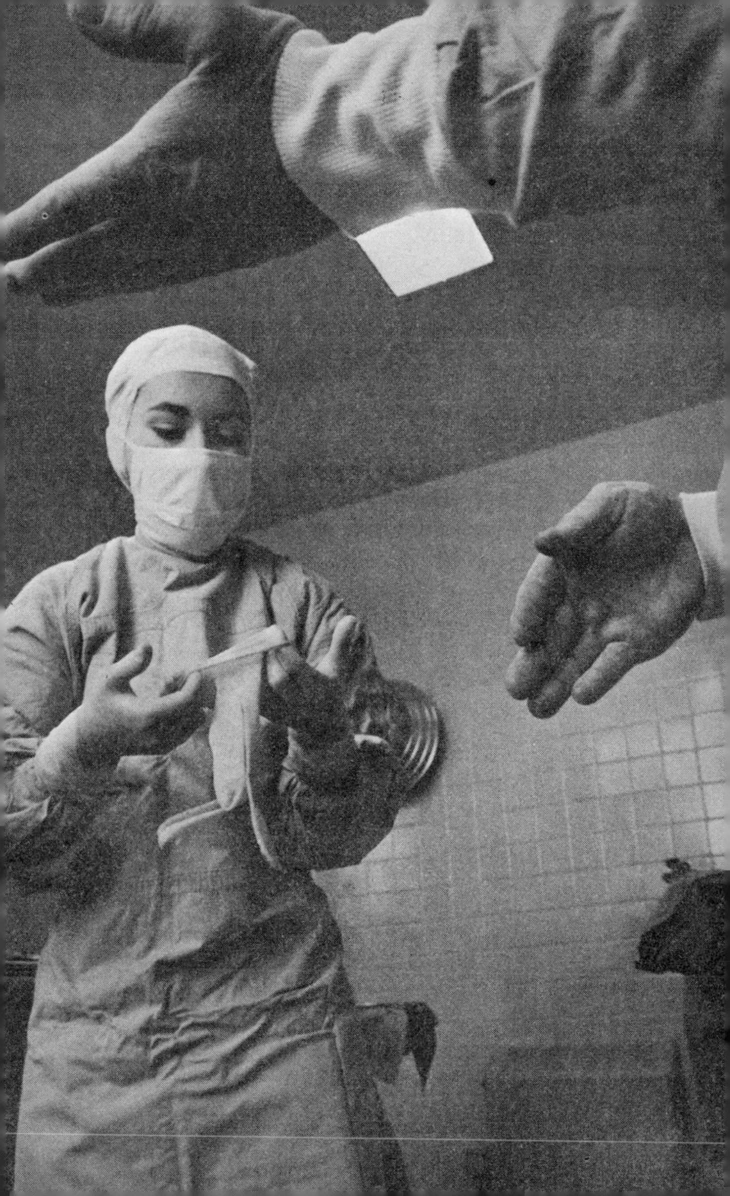

in the whole effort of our lives. Loving others means not only having a trusting faith in them and being open to their love; not only respecting them truly as persons rather than things and accepting their respect; not only allowing them room to be and to grow as their real selves. Loving also means to care and to serve, to be responsible to other people. It involves us in the discipline of loving service; it demands from us the patience of concentrated effort and dedication. Normally, gaining the satisfaction of the task well done can and should help us make this effort, to carry out what is involved in a dedication. And equally also, an essential aspect of our caring and serving must be the effort to do so more effectively—to increase our knowledge and skill so as to serve others better.

A mother caring for a sick child exemplifies a total quality of self-donation, knowing no limit of time, labor, weariness. (Such a mother also finds satisfaction in caring for her child, in making him more comfortable, in finally seeing him well. And a really devoted mother will find out from the doctor how to care for her child most effectively.) Many mothers and fathers exemplify complete dedication in their daily toil, caring for their families.

But all forms of work should be carried out in this spirit of maintaining the well-being of others. We expect to find dedicated nurses, doctors, teachers, clergymen, psychologists and social workers (those in the "service" professions). Yet the desire to serve others should be characteristic also of the lawyer, the executive, businessman, janitor, mechanic, truck driver. All work, to be truly human—let alone Christian—should contain some important element of service; it can and should always be a labor of love. Moreover, making work a labor of love may require, for the members of many professions, a lifetime of continued study and effort to make their service more effective.

Futher, our care for others must reach out beyond our homes and our own occupations to the needs of our neighbors, our community, our society, the whole world. We may exercise this care through personal efforts, through voting, through various types of organizations, but we must exercise it somehow if our love for God and neighbor is to have any reality. We cannot be indifferent to the needs of the underprivileged, the poor, the unemployed and unemployable. We must find positive, effective ways to support the efforts of people seeking to satisfy needs in our own communities and all over the world, if we are to obey God's command to love our neighbor.

The sight of love at work caring for others should help us to understand God's love and care for each of us. We should not accept this understanding lightly. For once we accept it in our hearts with some degree of mature understanding, our lives can never be the same. God's love has an infinite quality; it goes beyond the mature qualities of human loving discussed in this chapter; it goes beyond even all that is told of love in the Bible, limited as the written Word of God must be by human thought and expression.

Once we make the decision to commit ourselves to a full belief in this love, and to the fact that the

Spirit of this love is to animate our lives, we find ourselves dedicated to a personal response of total loving seemingly impossible in its demands. This requirement is put to us clearly by Jesus when He says: "A new commandment I give you, that you love one another: that as I have loved you, you also love one another" (John 13: 34).

Communists accuse Christians of promising needy people "pie in the sky when you die," instead of doing anything to help them. Some secular humanists feel very strongly that Christianity as it is mainly practiced in our society distracts Christians from the urgent concerns of mankind, from the service of their neighbors' needs. Clearly, we all need to learn better the lesson that loving means caring (in complete faith that the Holy Spirit will enable us to do so) if we are to give Christian witness in today's world. "We must love," as St. John says, "in deed and in truth" (1 John 3: 18).

READINGS: John 10; John 13: 1-35; Matthew 20: 20-34, 25: 31-46; Ephesians 4, 5; Colossians 3.

DISCUSSION QUESTIONS

Are the various kinds of work and professions carried out by the members of the group generally considered to be forms of loving service of neighbor? Could all of them be carried out in such a way? Would such a reorientation have any bearing on the reform of society called for by Pope John XXIII?

What forms of work in modern society are least suited to be carried out as forms of loving service of neighbor? Could automation help to eliminate at least one group of these?

How could parents best help their children to gain a proper human and Christian motivation for gaining their education? Do most students you know have such a motivation? If not, why not?

Are most of the Catholics you know, including priests and religious, aware that all Christians are called to a life of loving service of others? How might a wider diffusion of this ideal help to produce a greater number of solid priestly and religious vocations?

Do you think that the methods of religious instruction with which you are acquainted encourage the development of a truly Christian conscience? How might they be improved? How might parents be helped to guide their children more effectively in the development of a truly Christian conscience?

Do most of the Catholics you know understand love as meaning labor, service, dedication? How could this understanding best be developed in your parish?

What effect would a better understanding of what is involved in our duty to love our neighbor have in the work of your parish organizations? What effect might it have in your community? in our society?

> *God, who is rich in mercy, by reason of his very great love wherewith he has loved us, even when we were dead by reason of our sins, brought us to life together with Christ (by grace*

you have been saved) and raised us up together, and seated us together in heaven in Christ Jesus. For by grace you have been saved through faith; and that not from yourselves, for it is the gift of God; not as the outcome of works, lest anyone may boast. For his workmanship we are, created in Christ Jesus in good works, which God has made ready beforehand that we may walk in them.

Ephesians 2: 4-10

Chapter Five

IN LOVING WE DISCOVER OURSELVES

Now that faith has come, we are no longer under a tutor. For you are all the children of God through faith in Christ Jesus. For all of you have been baptized into Christ, have put on Christ. There is neither Jew nor Greek; there is neither slave nor freeman; there is neither male nor female. For you are all one in Christ Jesus. And if you are Christ's, then you are the offspring of Abraham, heirs according to promise.

Galatians 3: 25-29

All of us are concerned, at every stage in our lives, with the problem of the meaning of ourselves. Over and over again, at various crises in our lives, we ask ourselves afresh, "Who, really, am I? What will I be? What do other people think of me?" But the task of finding a consistent view of our own identity and of the meaning that we have for other people seems to be a particular characteristic of adolescence. For this reason, above all, the space of life between childhood and mature adulthood is usually a time of confusion and uncertainty.

During this period, perhaps more than any other, young people should be learning a great deal about the meaning of love if they are to grow toward true maturity. They need at the same time to adapt the earlier lessons to their new stage of growth, and learn new ones. As the lessons of loving are never very easily learned, we are not surprised that adolescence is such a difficult age.

At this stage also the mistakes made in early upbringing and growth become very evident; whatever inadequacies the young person may suffer in his achievement of trusting love, and in his achievement of the free and happy expression of a real self through initiative, commitment and responsibility, begin now to show their painful effects. For he must build and rebuild on the foundation laid earlier as he steps out of childhood and faces the task of finding his meaning as a grown person.

Adolescence is a time of rapid development—social, emotional, physical, sexual, and intellectual (and maturing does not necessarily take place harmoniously and evenly in all these areas). This development seems to demand from the young person a new personality and a new set of roles in life, vastly different from the familiar ones of childhood. He struggles for a new independence, and often shows this need by rebelliousness. Yet he wants to conform—not to his parents' norms, but to those of his peers. He wants to be accepted by his peers, to identify himself with them, and feels the need to enter into various new kinds of love-relationships.

One of these relationships, often very dominant, is that of hero worship—the idealization of a person, usually older and with whom one does not come in daily contact, combined with a strong desire not only to admire him from afar but somehow to relate oneself to him, to draw his personality into oneself and so to identify with him. Another relationship, quite normal to adolescence, is the "crush", which has less intellectual idealization but the same desire somehow to relate oneself to the person whom one has invested with desirable qualities—perhaps the ones apparently most lacking in oneself. Both these relationships are forms of love—immature forms, certainly, but very probably a kind of needed apprenticeship for the mature forms of friendship and married love.

The adolescent also feels deeply the need for real friendship with persons of the same sex, for a per-

COOL-RAY
BONANZA
BILLY THE KI
BLUE BEET
FIGHTIN' AIR FORCE
TARZAN
WOODY WOODPE
FIGHTIN' AIR FORCE

sonal and meaningful one-to-one relationship, deeper and more supporting than childhood companion-friendships or peer-group identification. Since friendship is a major form of mature love, it is a pity that, in our times, many adolescents and young men fear forming deep friendships with other men lest this be an indication of latent homosexuality. A similar fear also exists, though probably to a considerably lesser degree, in girls and young women.

Certainly, one of the major, if not *the* major, aspect of the adolescent's search for his own identity in relation to others is the search for the meaning of sex and its relationship to love. Boys, with their far stronger and clearer awakening sexual drives, need help in relating love as trust, commitment, responsibility, self-giving, to this new kind of desire. They tend, as an article in *Redbook* so well said, to play at love in order to get sex, whereas girls tend to play at sex in order to get love. Both need to be shown the existence and dangers of these two tendencies. They also need to be shown the possibility of work and friendship relationships with members of the opposite sex, and to be given ample opportunities for forming these, so that they do not meet the other sex only, or even mainly, under the conditions of dating.

Some young people, certainly, in spite of the vulgarity, cynicism and hypocritical puritanism with which they are surrounded, still manage to fall in love in the simple old-fashioned sense, discovering happily the meaning that a person of the other sex can have for them, and experiencing the beauty and joy of a face-to-face meeting with another in love.

This new level of loving can transform the whole of life; the boy or girl may be walking on air as if nothing in the world counts except love.

In this new vision of life as illuminated by love, temporary as the experience may be, the young person may find most clearly the new self-meaning which he has been searching for with so many hesitations. From the shattering experience of being fully loved for his very own self, by someone on whom he has no claim but love, he may find an increasingly confident vision of his own dignity and worth as a person, and his meaning and value to others.

If the adolescent is to achieve the full value of this experience and understand its full joy, he needs the support of everything that he has already learned about love as trust, commitment, responsibility, care and selfless dedication. Without such a many-sided appreciation of the meaning of loving another person fully, he may easily be guided by his unruly sexual feelings into premature sexual intercourse or early marriage. He may take for granted the incomplete union between sex and love that binds so many people together in immature relationships of one kind and another. Certainly, one of the chief tasks of adolescence is to begin to discover the meaning of sex in relation to love.

Obviously, then, young people of both sexes need far more adequate education in the meaning of sex and love than most of them are now being given by their parents, by their schools, and by the *mores* and mass media of our society. Otherwise some of them will never become capable of a mature com-

CREAM
MALTS
ICE CREAM

mitment to marriage, and of real friendship with persons of the same and of the opposite sex.

The task of parents and counselors of adolescents is certainly a very difficult one—and made far more difficult by the hypocritical standards and pressures of our society. They have to try to support and encourage the adolescent's positive efforts to grow, providing firm strength when he is weakened by his confused sense of self-determination and self-control, and sympathizing with him in his real difficulties.

Above all, parents and counselors must keep their lines of communication open with him, so that he may slowly and surely be convinced of their continuing, permanent love and regard for him. For, as in his first essays in independence as a small child, it is through his elders' daily, unchangeable love and respect for him as the person he is and is trying to become, that he can begin to gain a firm conviction of his own dignity and value as a person, of his own secure and consistent self-meaning.

Such respect and understanding, support and love are the more necessary for adolescents as they are increasingly faced with the necessity for making decisions about personal relationships and about study, work and vocation. Ideally, young people should increasingly perceive the implications of their decisions in terms of love; they should increasingly sense how their decisions affect their understanding of themselves, their relationships of love and friendship with others, and their love-relationship with God. They should be helped to make decisions, more and more consciously and realistically, in terms of God and man.

The idealism and the rebelliousness of youth often combine to lead young people away from the safe, well-placed ladders to success. They show mounting enthusiasm for causes. They join the Peace Corps. They take part in freedom marches. They want to ban the bomb, and to outlaw oppression, war, poverty and ignorance. And many of them give lavishly of their time and energy to carry out programs for the underprivileged.

Their determination can try the patience of the best parents, who feel better able to comprehend the demands and issues of the day, and point out to their young people that there can be no easy solution to current problems. The task of leading young people to a mature view of love, and to a realistic appreciation of love's demand for daily decision and commitment, is never an easy one. We older people must guard against the frustrated cynicism that comes so easily from our own failures to love, as expressed, for example, in such statements as: "What's the use? You can't change human nature." We have to be on guard against our tendencies to safeguard young people and make their decisions for them, forcing them into one or another of the "little boxes" that we might find congenial ourselves.

We need, above all, to help young people see that the Christian vocation, whatever its form, is a call to love according to God's plan. We need to help them gain a vision of this plan to gather human persons together in a community of love with one another and with Him—a community standing in a love-relationship to Christ analogous to the human relationships of marriage and friendship, a community called to the "glorious freedom of the sons of God" in the Spirit. We need to help them to see that, in consequence, all their human relationship can shed light on and foster their relationship to God, and that the love poured out in their hearts by the Holy Spirit can purify, deepen and carry beyond their limitations, all their human loves.

The adult feels most keenly his own inadequate understanding of love, his own weak commitment to make decisions in terms of love, and his own failures to love, when he tries to help the adolescent. Yet this feeling itself may help us to communicate with younger people effectively, if it leads us afresh to search out the love-meaning of our own lives, and to open ourselves to the love of Christ. Then the young people whom we are trying to help will sense our desire to do what we are asking them to do. They will sense our conviction that the love of Christ, dwelling in our inner being through the personal gift of His Spirit, can transform the whole of our lives and give them their ultimate meaning; that a life open to this dynamic energy of love can create in the person an ever-deeper understanding of who and what he is, and what he is meant to be for himself and other men.

READINGS: 1 Corinthians 12: 4-13, 13; Ephesians 4: 1-16; Philippians 2: 1-13.

DISCUSSION QUESTIONS:

In what ways does our society make adolescence unnecessarily difficult and frustrating? What could be done in a practical way to counterbalance these forces in families, parishes, communities?

Why do adolescents who have been deprived and those who have been pampered both tend to the same types of antisocial behavior?

Do you think it is very common for parents to project on their adolescent children their own anxieties and frustrations in love? Are there any ways in which adolescents could be helped to understand their parents as real persons?

Do you think that, within marriage, sexual intercourse as a function of deep interpersonal love is easy to accomplish?

What would you say to a young couple about nineteen years old who love one another very deeply, feel that they have committed themselves to one another for life, and are thinking of carrying out this commitment through sexual intercourse although they are not as yet able to marry?

If adolescents were given the opportunity to make more responsible decisions and, in general, to take on more responsibility in our society than they usually are, would this help them to go through adolescence more successfully and fruitfully? If so, how might such responsibilities be given to them in families, parishes, in schools, in communities?

Do many teenagers in your community give up the practice of religion? If so, for what reasons? Do you think the adolescent period should be the normal time for a young person to gain a deeper understanding of Christian faith and love?

Are parents in any way responsible for other parents' adolescent children? Are single people? If so, how should they exercise this responsibility?

> *When the Son of Man shall come in his majesty, and all the angels with him, then he will sit on the throne of his glory; and before him will be gathered all the nations, and he will separate them one from another, as the shepherd separates the sheep from the goats; and he will set the sheep on his right hand, but the goats on the left. Then the king will say to those on his right hand. Come, blessed of my Father, take possession of the kingdom prepared for you from the foundation of the world; for I was hungry and you gave me to eat; I was thirsty and you gave me to drink; I was a stranger and you took me in; naked and you covered me; sick and you visited me; I was in prison and you came to me. Then the just will answer him, saying, "Lord, when did we see thee hungry, and feed thee; or thirsty, and give thee drink? And when did we see thee a stranger, and take thee in; or naked, and clothe thee? Or when did we see thee sick, or in prison, and come to thee? And answering, the king will say to them, "Amen I say to you, as long as you did it for one of these, the least of my brethren, you did it for me."*
>
> Matthew 25: 31-40

Chapter Six

LOVING MEANS OVERCOMING ISOLATION

Happy are you who fear the Lord,
who walk in his ways!
For you shall eat the fruit of your handiwork;
happy shall you be, and favored.
Your wife shall be like a fruitful vine
in the recesses of your home;
Your children like olive plants
around your table.
Behold, thus is the man blessed
who fears the Lord.

The Lord bless you from Sion;
may you see the prosperity of Jerusalem
all the days of your life;
May you see your children's children.
Peace be upon Israel!

Psalm 127

When we attend a wedding we cannot help wondering what the couple's life together will bring them. We hear them saying that they accept one another for better or for worse, for richer or for poorer. How often have we seen their acceptance of each other turn out for the worse. How many couples, only a year or so after their marriage, look back to the happy days when they were single! Often, too, the human growth, happiness and love of couples seem to become less after marriage than when they were living alone. When the first enthusiasm of what they took to be love fades away, husband and wife can, indeed, be still more lonely than when they lived alone, even when their marriage itself survives. Why does that seem to happen so frequently?

All adult loving involves us in giving ourselves and accepting the reality of other persons in a much more total way than the friendships and loves of adolescence. The total quality of mature love sheds a penetrating light on our personality and reveals our inner meaning; the demand of active commitment calls on the resources of our innermost being. But many people avoid this deep look into themselves, brought on by the demands of mature love, and try, somewhat vainly, to make a success of marriage and of other forms of adult commitment through a shallow level of love and personal dedication.

Such a withdrawal may well be the effect of a person's failure to accept himself, to love himself. Because he does not find himself lovable, he shuts off his inner self from those closest to him, lest they should reject him if they could see him as he is. As we saw earlier, one major element in our maturing is the gradually increasing sense of being ourselves, separate and different from other persons. Through trusting in love, we grow in initiative and autonomy, forming our own ideals and standards, finding a consistent meaning and purpose of life in ourselves. Adutlhood gives us our final independence as persons, but also turns our concentration again on our own inner meaning. And then, if our sense of individuality, of self-possession and autonomy, is not to lead us into loneliness and isolation, it must lead us outward and onward into love.

If we are to meet the demand of mature love and its penetrating reality, we must first accept our own inner meaning, to love ourselves. This does not mean approving of all that we see in ourselves; on the contrary, the more we love ourselves truly, the more conscious we become of all our failures to love. Our capacity to give ourselves fully in love to another or to accept the other person's love for us depends upon our love for ourselves and our acceptance of ourselves as we are and as we hope to be.

Those who enter marriage without this growing capacity for giving themselves in love and without fully accepting the other person for what he or she is (rather than some idealized or quite different person) face the danger of centering their marriage on the immediate joy and pleasure of sexual intercourse. The very nature of the marriage act can itself have a liberating effect on each person, breaking through reserves of isolation and leading a couple into a deeper understanding and acceptance of the love-demand of their total daily life. But this is true only when a couple already possess at least some love-maturity and already have some idea of the intimate interpenetration of life and person that a marriage should gradually effect.

When a couple without this capacity and vision make sexual intercourse the focal interest and joy of their marriage, they may easily damage its real unity. A woman can begin to feel that her husband needs her for intercourse only. A husband can begin to feel neglected in his real self, and to tire of the familiarity of the sexual relationship with the same woman all the time. And each of them can gradually lapse into a state of sad loneliness and isolation.

The danger of self-isolation is very obvious in marriage, since marriage of its nature calls for the most complete self-giving and receiving possible between two human beings. But isolation is a tragedy within marriage or any state of life. As we achieve some individual independence and self-meaning, we easily conclude that self-sufficiency is the final goal of life, and forget that we have won this achievement of self only to be able to enter more freely and maturely into love. From babyhood on, we all suffer more or less acutely from negative urges which tend to isolate us from the love and warmheartedness of others. Suspicion, mistrust, self-deception, anxiety, and our various false fronts always tend to pull us into ourselves, to cause us to withdraw into isolation. We must all fight against these tendencies, and remain open to receive and to give love. Without daily, active loving, any life—married or single—becomes empty and sterile.

The situation of marriage itself can, and often does, force married people to discover the necessity for openness and warm-heartedness. But people who stay single may either not see this demand so vividly, or see it very urgently and not know what to do about it, thinking that love has passed them by. They may conclude that nothing more is required of them than loving their neighbor in the rather vague sense of not really hating anyone. We all know people who have settled for such a pale way of living—lonely bachelors and spinsters in their thirties and forties who, however busy and popular they may seem to be, lead withdrawn lives of quiet anxiety and frustration.

For nothing could be a greater tragedy in life than to cease growing in love, and to think that one's state of life does not require love. Whether a young adult deliberately chooses to stay single, or just does not find the right partner for marriage, he or she must be building a growing capacity for love in all he does or plans. He must be loving, daily and actively, or he will gradually wither.

As we saw earlier, one's work itself should be a form of loving, through serving others lovingly. Aside from work, the unmarried are much freer than most married people to consider what needs exist among their own relatives, in their church community, in the community of their town or city, in their country and the world, and to undertake whatever form of service is best suited to their talents and circumstances.

But, over and above what the unmarried person is able to do for others (though mainly, perhaps, in the context of this loving service), he or she needs to cultivate many real interpersonal relationships of friendship, both with members of the same and of the opposite sex. There may, obviously, be dangers in some of these relationships; they can never take on any aspect of the exclusive and total character of the commitment of marriage and still remain creatively loving. Adults should certainly remain aware of and guard against these dangers but never be so intimidated by them that they fall into a withdrawing attitude, afraid of approaching others with love.

In the same way, married people also need to cultivate interpersonal relationships; husband and wife cannot be "all in all to one another" in the sense of exhausting one another's capacity for friendship. Within the context of married life and in due proportion to its demands, being very careful to keep their marriage relationship central in their loving, both husband and wife need to make, and to continue to make, real friends.

Christians are bound, moreover, into a close fellowship of men and women pledged to live by the love of Christ, in His Spirit. This community of love needs seriously to be made a visible reality today, a "sacrament" of God's love, by incarnating it in open groups of Christian men and women, united by common interests and concerns and by Christian affection for one another as well. Both single persons and married couples can become the focal points of such groups, which can help so greatly to provide the climate of affection which the adult, as well as the child, needs if he is to continue to mature, and which modern society is so deficient in providing.

In choosing one's state of life and kind of work, then, primary consideration should be given to the question: "How can I best grow in love? How can I serve God and my fellowmen most lovingly?" Some people, for example, have chosen a profession —art, teaching, social work—which seems to demand of them such a total dedication that marriage and a family are out of the question. Such persons might well look into themselves to be sure that their decision not to marry is really based on love, not on withdrawal from love, on ambition, self-importance, or an urge to dominate others.

In a special way, those who dedicate themselves in the priesthood, sisterhood, or brotherhood, need to be very sure that theirs is a dedication of active loving, not one of either withdrawal or ambition or a need for security. The only justification for the celibacy of priests and religious is that it be understood and lived, not as a negation of love, but as a more total and demanding challenge to love and serve. The Church expresses this aim in the liturgy for the Profession of nuns: "You have willed that chosen souls of loftier purpose should reject the bodily intercourse of men and women, but attain the secret that it comprehends; who do not copy what marriage does, but devote their whole love to the mystery which is signifies."

This mystery of love is the love of Christ for His Church, of which marriage is a sacramental sign.

"Husbands, love your wives," St. Paul writes, "just as Christ also loved the Church and delivered himself up for her, that he might sanctify her, cleansing her in the bath of water by means of the word: in order that he might present to himself the Church in all her glory, not having spot or wrinkle, or any such thing, but that she might be holy and without blemish" (Ephesians 5: 25-27).

All the member of the Church share in this union of the Church with Christ; all are called, in one way or another, to live out in their lives this mystery of love. All are called to take part in Christ's work of gathering human persons together in a community of love with one another and with God, until every shadow of loneliness will fade in the light of the eternal marriage feast. "I saw the holy city, New Jerusalem, coming down out of heaven from God, made ready as a bride adorned for her husband. And I heard a loud voice from the throne saying, 'Behold the dwelling of God with men, and he will dwell with them. And they will be his people, and God himself will be with them as their God. And God will wipe away every tear from their eyes. And death shall be no more; neither shall there be mourning, nor crying, nor pain any more, for the former things have passed away.' " (Apocalypse 21: 2-4).

Here and now, in the community of the Church, we can meet Christ in the signs of His continuing love called the sacraments. Each of the sacramental signs gives us an added gift and assurance of His love within us, supporting and energizing us in every need of our life.

The sacraments, especially the Holy Eucharist,

are also the signs of our united community response of love to the Father; through them our small and failing efforts of daily loving are swept up into the love of Christ for His Father. Taking part in the celebration of the Eucharist, then, can and should, in our lives, as in the life of the whole Church, be the climax and the source of our efforts to love, to respond to God's call to be "imitators of God, as very dear children, and walk in love, as Christ also loved us and delivered himself up for us as an offering and a sacrifice to God to ascend in fragrant odor" (Ephesians 5: 1-2).

READINGS: Psalm 121; Ephesians 5: 1-32; Colossians 4: 12-17; Romans 12.

DISCUSSION QUESTIONS:

What do you think indicates that a person has passed from adolescence to adulthood?

Do you think many young people you know marry too soon? What are the advantages of early marriage? the disadvantages?

In what ways should a mature attitude to love show itself in the day-to-day affairs of married life and in carrying out the marriage act? in the lives of single people? in lives of dedicated virginity and celibacy?

Do you think that many single people, say in their thirties, tend to feel lonely and neglected? If so, what could be done about it—by themselves? by others?

Do you think our society tends to foster isolation

of persons from one another? If so, what might be done about it in your parish or community?

In what way are the sacraments signs of Christ's love? Do you think that most Catholics think of them merely as "means of grace"? What might be wrong or limited about this attitude?

Can our whole life, everything we are and everything we do, become a daily offering of love to God? What practical demands would this make on people like yourselves? Is this an impossible ideal for ordinary men and women?

> *For the love of Christ impels us, because we have come to the conclusion that, since one died for all, therefore all died; and that Christ died for all, in order that they who are alive may live no longer for themselves, but for him who died for them and rose again. So that henceforth we know no one according to the flesh. And even though we have known Christ according to the flesh, yet now we know him so no longer. If then any man is in Christ, he is a new creature; the former things have passed away; behold, they are made new!*
>
> 2 Corinthians 5: 14-18

Chapter Seven

LOVING IS CREATIVE GENEROSITY

And he himself gave some men as apostoles, and some as prophets, others again as evangelists, and others as pastors and teachers, in order to perfect the saints for a work of ministry, for building up the body of Christ, until we all attain to the unity of the faith and of the deep knowledge of the Son of God, to perfect manhood, to the mature measure of the fullness of Christ. And this he has done that we may be now no longer children, tossed to and fro and carried about by every wind of doctrine devised in the wickedness of men, in craftiness, according to the wiles of error. Rather are we to practice the truth in love, and so grow up in all things in him who is the head, Christ. For from him the whole body (being closely joined and knit together through every joint of the system according to the functioning in due measure of each single part) derives its increase to the building up of itself in love.

Ephesians 4: 11-16

As little children, we begin to love because of what we receive from love. Through childhood and adolescence, we should slowly come to realize that love means giving as well as receiving, a two-way generosity leading eventually to a true meeting of persons. In adult life we must take a further step in love and discover that, when two mature persons love one another, they begin to reach out in generosity beyond themselves. Mature love must overflow to others.

As we saw earlier, even small children begin to grasp what sharing love with others means. They can come to understand that their mother does not love them any the less because she also gives her love to their father and to the other children. But this sense of love as something to be shared grows only very slowly. (This is one reason why brothers and sisters frequently have trouble getting along with one another. A girl in her late teens, for example, who begins to love her little brother as a real person shows genuine maturity.) We all tend, more or less, to be exclusive, to feel, for example, that when a third person joins a conversation with an intimate friend, something precious has been lost. But, in any relationship, when "giving up" exclusiveness is achieved with generosity, we gain rather than lose; the close intimacy of two is enriched with a new joy and permanence. For love must be generously creative if it is to grow, or even endure.

This truth has not dawned on those married couples who fear that a baby may threaten their mutual love. In many such cases, the partners have not fully outgrown the competitive attitudes of childhood days. They should be thinking of their baby, not as a competitor for love, but as a sign and gift of new life their love should always create. Indeed, married love can and should be creative in many ways—not only by bringing new human beings into existence, but also through whatever the couple do, together or separately, to serve God and their fellowmen. Childless couples, therefore need not feel denied of the creativity of love; they need, rather, to see how they can best exercise love's creativity.

Without some creative overflowing, the mutual love of any two people risks the death of mutual selfishness. When two children are playing and a third child comes along, for instance, he may be told, "Go away! This is just for the two of us—we don't want anyone else." In small children, such selfishness is normal; among adults, whether they be married or close friends, this attitude is a tragedy. Such mutually sanctioned selfishness, even if unconscious, stifles love.

Thus, love must be creative and outgoing, for both single and married people. Whatever may be the ways they have chosen to center their lives in love, they must guard against any narrowing of love by "keeping it just for ourselves." This may be encountered by those in the various "helping professions," for example, if they are not properly trained

and alert to the possibility that this exclusive attitude may be adopted either by themselves or by those whom they are trying to help.

Those who choose a celibate vocation of service within the Church are, obviously, not exempt from this danger. Their celibacy is meant to be a living sign of the creative and ever-welcoming love of the Holy Spirit; the selfish and exclusive are not authentic celibates. The selfish, exclusive attitude will often be rationalized as a devoted concern for the needs of one's own task, for the growth of one's own parish, school, or religious order. But anything that arbitrarily sets limits to overflowing generosity proper to love cannot ultimately benefit the Body of Christ, which must "build itself up in love."

Our loving must, at every stage of our lives, be generous and overflowing if we are not to wither up. When we approach middle age, we begin to realize, in one way or another, how selfishness withers the person, and how much we may have missed of the growth of love in our lives. The middle-aged can hardly help reappraising themselves: "Where am I going? Am I on the right way there?"

When they are young, many people enter marriage, the religious life, the priesthood, or a service profession, on a wave of high idealism. They go along for some years reasonably content with themselves and with their practice of the Christian life. They become confident in their mastery of the art of loving, certain they are truly in love with what they wanted to be and to do. But as they try to live out their life commitments, their confidence and idealism is severely tested by the demands of reality, by the requirements of love in daily action.

Such people may conclude, by the time they reach middle age, that the glory and joy of loving which they hoped to find in their chosen vocation was only a fairy tale for the young; that life is actually very much a matter of every man for himself. We meet such persons all too often—persons who, though they once had an idealistic life-commitment, seem to have settled for simply hanging on, or getting ahead.

Yet, at middle age or any age, we can allow a fresh awareness of the realities of life to become the occasion for a new look at ourselves in the light of the Spirit of truth. We may well conclude that, in spite of our high ideals and our dedication, we have not yet learned the primary lessons of loving—that we lack basic trust in ourselves, in others, and in God; that we have never really worked at building up the Body of Christ in love; that our relations with others and with God have been largely based on self-interest.

Such a view of ourselves need be no cause for discouragement. It may rather be the sign of a maturing Christian conscience, beginning to see and judge in terms of Christian love rather than of punctiliously fulfilling duties. For a Christian conscience must mature slowly, at the pace of our growth in understanding love.

A little child's self-understanding and self-judgment are, naturally expressed in terms of his self-absorbed need to be loved; they express themselves in an anxiety about what others may do to him if he does what is forbidden. Too frequently, in later childhood and adolescence, the Christian life is still put before him in the same terms of childish self-interest, and little encouragement is given to the growth of his new life as a Christian acting with others, concerned with the creative demands of outward loving. So conscience can appear to him as an unwanted companion, enforcing on him a series of narrow prohibitions and an uneasy anxiety about violating them.

Many of us were brought up with this notion of conscience. But the whole spirit and message of the renewal now taking place in the Church is a renewal of growth, of cooperation with the Spirit of truth to bring our consciences to true Christian maturity. For we are never too old to begin to love; every step forward in love is a new beginning, the growth of new life. Love is always creative, particularly the Love of God, the Holy Spirit, who is the Spirit at once of love and truth.

Ideally, all of us should have grown in love as we grew in age; this is the ideal of education, but one mainly unrealized in man's present condition. Genuine loving does not come easily; we do not grow towards mature love inevitably. We seem always to be fighting against constricting forces of anxiety, suspicion, apathy and confusion. We seem to be prisoners, slaves to the worst part of our nature. We may realize that our only liberation, our only way to freedom, is to learn how truly to love. But this may seem beyond our reach.

God's message to us in Christ is the good news of our liberation from this human condition of self-slavery. Jesus preached freedom from self-slavery to His own townsfolk at Nazareth: "The Spirit of God is upon me . . . to proclaim to the captives release" (Luke 4: 14-20). Through Jesus, God reveals in love the meaning of all reality, the inner meaning of our lives. He lets us see Himself as love personified, a threefold interpersonal loving which is the dynamic center and destiny of all that is. The Son comes into our world, accepting our human condition fully so as to liberate us from within by His acts of love, and to offer us His own Spirit of truth and love as a free gift from the Father.

When we accept this gift with trusting faith, we enter into the love-fellowship of those pledged to "live by the Spirit." This creative Spirit of Jesus comes to be the central energy of our lives, helping us to grow in freedom, truth and love. If then, at any period in our lives, we are beginning to see our own failure and inadequacy in love, this may be the work of the Spirit within us, leading us to mature self-understanding as the only basis on which love can gain its full creative power in our lives.

We should be able to find, at such a crisis of growth, a deep support in the whole fellowship of the Church, united in the Spirit of Christ. Its active community life of charity and generosity, its teaching which daily takes us back to the New Testament message, and its sacramental liturgy, should all give support and sustenance to a new life of love and freedom in the truth of the Spirit. The gift of the Spirit does not take away from us, this side of death, the constant daily struggle of growth against apathy and evil; nor does the gift of the Spirit within the fellowship of the Church, and its union of love with Christ, take away the element of human fault and failure in the Church-community and the need for its daily struggle towards new life and growth. But to each of us personally, and to the whole Church, God daily offers new light, new energy, more penetrating standards of self-judgment, and an inner urge to love as Christ loves.

We all need to accept more completely the challenge of this new level of loving; it will not drive any genuine love out of our lives, but will make the whole effort of our loving creative beyond our dreams, for it will be united with the ultimate creative love of the Spirit of God.

READINGS: Romans 12, 13; 2 Corinthians 6: 1-10; Philippians 2; 1 John 3, 4.

DISCUSSION QUESTIONS:

Discuss the ways in which the love of two persons should reach out beyond themselves. To what extent can this be true of every family—whether the couple have children or not? In what ways might a family express that it is a community of love?

How might the creative force of love become a reality in the community of your neighborhood? of your city? Do you think it is a practical ideal for every human community to be a fellowship of love? How would this apply in practice to colleges, prisons, clubs, nations, the whole human family?

Do you think that the Church in your area is operating as a fellowship of divine love? What has been achieved towards this ideal? Where has there been failure? What steps forward could be taken? What might you do about it as a member of this fellowship?

Is the idea of Christian conscience outlined in this chapter very common among the Christians you know? By what signs would you judge this?

Does the Christian message get through to your generation as the good news of love, truth, freedom? Do you find this view of Christianity common among Christians? Among non-Christians?

What can any one person, or group, do to convince non-Christians of the real nature of the "Good News"?

> *As regards your former manner of life you are to put off the old man, which is being corrupted through its deceptive lusts. But he renewed in the spirit of your mind, and put on the new man, which has been created according to God in justice and holiness of truth. Wherefore, put away lying and speak truth each one to his neighbor, because we are members of one another. "Be angry and do not sin": do not let the sun go down upon your anger; do not give place to the devil. He who was wont to steal, let him steal no longer; but rather let him labor, working with his hands at what is good, that he may have something to share with him who suffers need. Let no ill speech proceed from your mouth, but whatever is good for sup-*

plying what fits in with the current necessity, that it may give grace to the hearers. And do not grieve the Holy Spirit of God, in whom you were sealed for the day of redemption. Let all bitterness, and wrath, and indignation, and clamor, and reviling, be removed from you, along with all malice. On the contrary, be kind to one another, and merciful, generously forgiving one another, as also God in Christ has generously forgiven you.

Ephesians 4: 21-32

Chapter Eight

LOVING IS FACING REALITY

But when the goodness and kindness of God our Savior appeared, then not by reason of good works that we did ourselves, but according to his mercy, he saved us through the bath of regeneration and renewal by the Holy Spirit, whom he has abundantly poured out upon us through Jesus Christ, our Savior, in order that, justified by his grace, we may be heirs in the hope of life everlasting.

Titus 3: 4-7

Not so long ago, most people made two false assumptions about life; one, personality growth inevitably slows down and ceases as does bodily growth; two, whatever maturity a person might have attained wanes and fades into childish senility as physical strength slopes down towards death.

We have all heard sayings like, "You can't teach an old dog new tricks" and "Of course, we can't expect older people to like changes." But nowadays we are becoming much more aware of the possibilities of new personality growth in middle age and old age. My own work as a prison chaplain and a marriage counselor has proved to me the value of later years, when people can really grow in the ways of love and find a richer meaning for their lives.

When men and women reach middle life, much of the urgent striving of their earlier days may well be over. Physical changes and increasing discomforts and ailments warn them of the dawning second half of life. Most middle-aged people who stop and reflect wonder what they would do if they had their lives to live over again. But as old age creeps inexorably on, they know that their time is running out. In retrospect, their life achievement can seem small, and the mistakes loom large.

Such self-doubt, with its tendency towards despondency and despair, can be a very real test of love in middle and old age. In our younger years, we can occupy ourselves with doing things, going places, meeting people, getting on, making money. The whirl of activity in our lives can keep our attention away from our doubts about ourselves and the significance of our life. But the excitement of all this striving fades with the passing years, at least for most people.

We are left face to face with ourselves and with the meaning of our lives. We seem to have to begin the task of loving almost all over again. Something in us seems to be dying; we have to give up some of the warm and comfortable ways of loving and striving and doing to which we have become accustomed, and go onwards into a deeper way of living and loving. We never seem done with growing in love; love is always leading us into new life, demanding the death of our old ways.

The new growth that later age demands is love's final integration of our life, and the full achievement of trust, acceptance and self-donation. Love is always a unifying force; it binds people together into one. It binds together the baby and the mother, children with parents and with brothers and sisters; it binds friends with friends, husband with wife, teacher with pupil, nurse with patient. It can bind, too, the scattered activities and energies of our personal life into one meaningful pattern. Love's integrating energy works in us all the time, but reaches its climax, its time of crisis, in our later years. Love in our final years must find for us the peace and serenity to face the end of life as we know it in faith and hope.

The steady, daily effort of loving gains for us

this final self-confidence and peace. Only with this effort comes the serene conviction of the final meaning of life: love. So we must continue, against our doubts, to be open to love in a final acceptance of reality. Only by continuing to love can we come to see—through and beyond the constant struggle to be loving persons, through and beyond the testing and the tensions, through and beyond the effort and hard work, through and beyond all the fun and joy of loving—that love is eventually our final acceptance of what is.

We must come to accept fully the reality of ourselves, with our gifts, ideals, and failures, with our achievements and our faults. We have always been loved, and always will be. Our response, in all truth, has been little enough. We must accept, too, the full reality of others, seeing them as they are or hope to be. We may wonder how often we have tried to make others over into puppets who would dance to our bidding and exist for our pleasure. Only late in life may we come to know love as helping the other person to be fully himself.

In late life we may also trustfully accept the real world; we finally put away our daydreams and our castles in the air, perhaps even some of the stirring causes and slogans of earlier life. We must come to trust ourselves to the world of real existence, marred as it is by man's greed and his failure to love.

The final growth of love brings us, then, face to face with reality. Our whole growth in love, from babyhood on, leads to final acceptance and openness; if in growing we see ourselves and our strivings as very small before God and His creation, we

enter into a basic Christian attitude of love. Only then can we praise the greatness of God in His creation and redemption with Our Lady as she does so strikingly in her Magnificat hymn (Luke 1: 46-55).

The full integrating energy of love helps us to draw together the scattered fragments of our living and loving. Events in our lives and attitudes of people toward us come together to unify the meaning of love and care.

While many things may still not fit in easily—elements of suffering, of sin, of hatred—the overall pattern gradually becomes clear. We can come to see, however dimly, our whole life as a gift of love. We can come to see love as the very shape of reality, the inner meaning and energy of all that is.

That this realization may finally dawn on a person in old age came to me recently with great force. I had been giving a lecture at our local university on the growth of conscience in children. Afterwards, an old man of almost ninety, who had taught me long ago and had been a professor of psychology most of his working life, came up to give me his comments. He said, "I've spent most of my life searching for the truth about human beings, and passing on whatever little wisdom I've gained; now, at the end, I'm seeing more and more that it all has to do with love, and that the key to it all is in the New Testament."

He had never been known as a religious man, so I told him that he was not the first old man to come to this conclusion. St. John the Apostle himself, when he was about the same age as my old friend, used to be carried (so his disciple St. Polycarp tells us) into church each Sunday, where he would always preach the same one-sentence sermon: "Children, love one another." When asked why he did this, he replied, "Because this is the Lord's command; nothing more is necessary."

Love is indeed the central theme of the Lord's message to us in the Bible. We see it in the story of creation, in the life of Abraham, in the Exodus, in the Psalms, and in the prophets; we find it poetically expressed in the love-themes of the Song of Songs. In the New Testament the whole meaning of Christ—His coming to be a man, His life, His death, and His new life after death—is all summed up in terms of love.

As we grow older we should frequently read St. John's account of the Last Supper (13-17). He begins on the theme of love: "Jesus, knowing that the time had come for him to pass out of this world to the Father, having loved his own who were in the world, loved them to the end" (John 13: 1). Here we discover the final meaning of our own lives reflected in the inner meaning of the life of Jesus Himself. We find our own truth and destiny shown in Christ's revelation of Himself to His Apostles. Here we are told of the gift of the Spirit, who will give us a new life based on truth and love; with the new life of Jesus we will one day pass through the gateway of death to the Father.

The new life of Christian love leads us fully to accept reality and brings us into final union with one another and with God. If we accept the Lord's message in our hearts with trusting faith, we shall find ourselves among those for whom Jesus prayed to His Father that night: "Yet not for these only do I pray, but for those also who through their word are to believe in me, that all may be one, even as thou, Father, in me and I in thee; that they also may be one in us, that the world may believe that thou hast sent me. And the glory that thou hast given me, I have given to them, that they may be one, even as we are one: I in them and thou in me; that they may be perfected in unity, and that the world may know that thou hast sent me, and that thou hast loved them even as thou hast loved me. Father, I will that where I am, they also whom thou hast given me may be with me; in order that they may behold my glory, which thou hast given me, because thou hast loved me before the creation of the world" (John 17: 20-24).

The remainder of the New Testament is like a practical commentary on and application of this prayer. It is summed up beautifully in St. Paul's prayer for the Christians of his own day and for us: "I bend my knees to the Father of our Lord Jesus Christ, from whom all fatherhood in heaven and on earth receives its name, that he may grant you from his glorious riches to be strengthened with power through his Spirit unto the progress of the inner man; and to have Christ dwelling through faith in your hearts; so that, being rooted and grounded in love, you may be able to comprehend with all the saints what is the breadth and length and height and depth, and to know Christ's love which surpasses knowledge, in order that you may be filled unto all the fullness of God" (Ephesians 3: 14-19).

Here, then, is the fulfillment of our growth in love. All who accept love in the full truth of reality, and give themselves fully in genuine loving, will find the utimate meaning of love in Christ and in the gift of His Spirit. The power of love, the creative energy of all reality, will carry us through death into the full enjoyment of new life and loving in the Risen Christ. So our death, far from being an end to our growing, will be still another new beginning, demanding from us the trustful confidence needed to leave behind the warm security of old ways, and to dare to enter, with full, open-hearted acceptance of reality, into a new, more intense joy of love without end.

READINGS: 1 Corinthians 13; John 13-17.

DISCUSSION QUESTIONS:

Do you think that the middle-aged and older people you know feel lost and lonely when their active days seem to fade? Could younger people be more understanding and helpful to them? In what ways?

What ideas would you have for a fifty-year old man or woman who feels that life no longer has much meaning or purpose?

Do you think that adolescents are capable of understanding much of the Christian meaning of love, life, and death outlined in this chapter? In what way could their taking part in the Mass help them towards this understanding?

Do you feel that the customs surrounding death and burial in your parish and local community adequately express the Christian message of love and hope?

What part of the New Testament best expresses for you personally the Christian meaning of life and love?

How could you help a person of your own age who feels that life is not worth living, that maybe suicide would be the best way out if one had the courage?

How does the theme of this book relate to the first book of the Christian Experience Series, "Through Death to Life"?

> *Who shall separate us from the love of Christ? Shall tribulation, or distress, or persecution, or hunger, or nakedness, or danger, or the sword? Even as it is written, "For thy sake we are put to death all the day long. We are regarded as sheep for the slaughter." But in all these things we overcome because of him who has loved us. For I am sure that neither death, nor life, nor angels, nor principalities, nor things present, nor things to come, nor powers, nor height, nor depth, nor any other creature will be able to separate us from the love of God, which is in Christ Jesus Our Lord.*
>
> Romans 8: 35-39

APPENDIX A

SUGGESTIONS FOR HOLDING A FRUITFUL DISCUSSION

Before the group meets, each member (or at least a majority of them) should have read the assigned chapter and the suggested Bible passages. To start the discussion, one member might be asked to give a brief summary of the chapter and of his reactions to it. After the discussion arising from this summary, the group could go on to consider the discussion questions given at the end of the chapter.

The members of the group should be quite clear as to the purpose of the discussion—to share their insights with one another, to help and to be helped to clarify their thinking and to widen their horizons.* A good discussion is a kind of love-feast in which ideas, rather than food, are shared. But a discussion of Christian attitudes toward death and life, to be really fruitful, will require a greater degree of openness among the participants, a greater degree of trust of one another, than a purely intellectual discussion —say of foreign or domestic policy—would call for. Each participant must be willing to contribute something from his own experience to make the discussion worthwhile.

The next necessity is that of not feeling in any way under pressure. No one should ever feel "put on the spot" or forced to try to contribute to the discussion of a given point when he really has nothing to say. Everyone should also feel free to digress or say something light and amusingly off-hand; there is no reason for a deadly seriousness. Naturally, the tendency to digress can be dangerous and should be curbed—but primarily by the participants, not by any one person in authority. Anyone who has nothing to say should feel perfectly free to pass the topic on to the next participant easily and comfortably. Certainly, no one should ever give the effect of *trying* to be brilliant or epigrammatic—or, for that matter, anything else.

During the first part of a discussion session with a large group (say, for the first half hour if the discussion is to go on for an hour and a half), it is well to limit the number of discussants to five. This number is large enough to insure a variety of contributors, with their different background, education, and points of view, and small enough to insure unity, depth, orderliness, and mobility of discussion.

When five are taken out of a large group and asked to handle a topic, they stimulate the others, who are sitting by and listening, to form their own opinions and to wish to express their ideas. When the five original discussants have finished, then there should be a break of five minutes or so in which the whole group can relax, think over and discuss with their neighbors what has been said. The discussion should then be thrown open to the whole group. This general discussion period should be used for commenting on, continuing, supplementing, and enriching what has already been said. It should, obviously, not be used for small stump speeches, and certainly not for any "attack" on one of the five original discussants. Here, too, contributions—additions and clarifications—are what are called for, not critical remarks. A very profitable method that can be followed by five participants is the following:

Let each person take the topic as it is passed to him, comment on it, and then pass it on, not to his immediate neighbor but to the person just beyond his immediate neighbor. Concretely, participant 1, having received and commented on the topic, should pass it on to participant 3; 3 does the same and passes it on to 5; 5 to 2; 2 to 4; and 4 back to one.

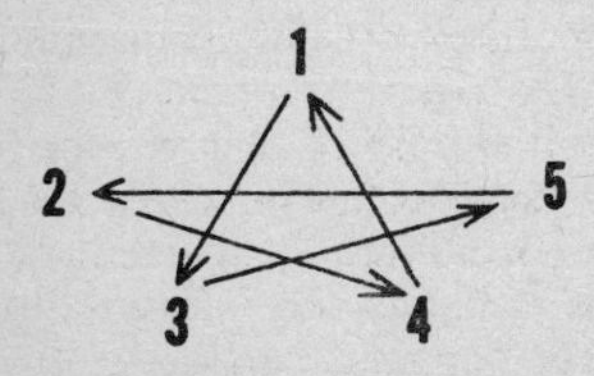

This procedure ensures varied, orderly, and easy discussion, provided the following rules are obeyed:

a) There should be no break in the order of procedure; no interruptions; no lengthy interchanges; no bickering or arguing. Thus when 1 receives the topic, he makes his statement about it and then passes the topic on to 3; only 3 can then comment on it. The interchange between 1 and 3 should be limited to a couple of sentences each. Anyone who takes exception to, or wishes to modify or comment on what 1 and 3 have said must wait his turn to do so—as they must if they wish, in turn, to comment on his ideas. Anyone can return to an earlier point for amplification at any time.

b) There should be frequent summaries of what the participants have said up to any given moment in the discussion. This mirroring or summarizing should not necessarily revolve on one person alone; everyone should feel responsible for keeping the discussion on—going and fruitful. Whoever does summarize should think of himself, not as a leader, but as a reflector or suggestion-maker.

c) The group should feel that it has the right to start all over again if the discussion is getting nowhere or is, in some way, bogged down.

This small group to large group procedure, and the method outlined of conducting the small group's discussion have been used successfully in many different situations. It has the advantage of opening up the subject without putting undue strain on any one person, and without the waste of time and embarrassment that come when no one feels like making the first remark. When it is used in discussions based on this booklet, one member of the group might still give the brief summary of the assigned chapter and his reactions to it, as suggested earlier, and the group of five take off from there, going on as indicated to the discussion questions.

But this procedure may not be necessary at all, especially when a group is not too large, and when the members have come to know one another well enough to feel free to express themselves and to offer truly creative listening, as well as verbal contributions to the progress of the discussion. The main thing is that the members come to feel that, through their discussions, they are helping one another and are being helped, at least in some degree, "to grow up *together* in him who is the head, Christ."

APPENDIX B

BIBLIOGRAPHY

Ahern, Barnabas Mary, LIFE IN CHRIST (pamphlet, Paulist Press, N. Y.). An excellent summary, in Scriptural terms, of the Christian life as a call to love.

Bowlby, John, MATERNAL CARE AND MENTAL HEALTH (International Documentary Service, Columbia University Press, N. Y.). In short form: CHILD CARE AND THE GROWTH OF LOVE (Penguin). The classic medical view of the effects and prevention of maternal deprivation; important for social workers, in children's institutions and child placement centers.

D'Arcy, Martin, THE MIND AND HEART OF LOVE (Meridian Books, N. Y.). A scholarly work giving a philosopher's view on theories of love from the Greeks through the existentialists. Rather lacking in unity and synthesis.

Erikson, Erik J., IDENTITY AND THE LIFE CYCLE (International Universities Press, N. Y.). The mature view of an ego psychologist on the process of human development; explains in detail his epigenetic principle of growth, and his eight stages which have formed a loose framework for this booklet.

Fromm, Erich, THE ART OF LOVING (Bantam Books). A small book, easily read, with viewpoints from psychology, social philosophy and religion. Presents very clearly the essential unity of love in human beings.

Haring, Bernard, GOD'S WORD AND MAN'S RESPONSE (pamphlet, Paulist Press, N. Y.). Christian morality as our response to God's love.

Lepp, Ignace, THE PSYCHOLOGY OF LOVING (Helicon, Baltimore). A penetrating picture of love and it's deviations by a depth psychologist; gives constructive criticism of many Christian misunderstandings and distortions in the area of love and sex. Presents little overall unity and synthesis.

Lewis, C. S., THE FOUR LOVES (Harcourt, N. Y.). The disunity of this work is suggested by the title, referring to Affection, Friendship, Eros, and Charity. However, it presents many insights from the viewpoint of a mature Christian philosopher.

Monden, Louis, SIN, LIBERTY, AND LAW (Sheed & Ward, N. Y.). A fresh and positive presentation of the essence of Christian morality, and the development of the Christian conscience.

Oraison, Marc, LOVE OR CONSTRAINT (Paulist Press, N. Y.). UNION AND MARITAL LOVE (The MacMillan Co., N. Y.). Straight forward, brilliant thinking in both these books by a priest-psychiatrist working in a Freudian framework. Deals with love from the viewpoints of the religious formation of children, and the physical and spiritual relationships of marriage.

Schnakenburg, Rudolf, THE MORAL TEACHING OF THE NEW TESTAMENT (Herder & Herder, N. Y.). A scholarly but very readable study.

Teilhard de Chardin, Pierre, THE DIVINE MILIEU (Harper & Row, N. Y.). One of the influential books of our time, giving a view of our life and growth in the creative love of Christ.

Tillich, Paul, THE NEW BEING (Scribner's, N. Y.). Clear, readable and penetrating sermon-essays by a modern theologian, dealing with our life in Christ as love, freedom, and fulfillment.